TERRORISM

AN INTERDISCIPLINARY PERSPECTIVE

Third Edition

D1277229

TERRORISM

AN INTERDISCIPLINARY
PERSPECTIVE

Third Edition

Edited by
Wadsworth/Thomson Learning

THOMSON
WADSWORTH

Australia • Canada • Mexico • Singapore • Spain • United Kingdom • United States

COPYRIGHT © 2004 Wadsworth, a division of
Thomson Learning, Inc. Thomson Learning™ is a
trademark used herein under license.

ALL RIGHTS RESERVED. No part of this work
covered by the copyright hereon may be reproduced
or used in any form or by any means—graphic,
electronic, or mechanical, including but not limited to
photocopying, recording, taping, Web distribution,
information networks, or information storage and
retrieval systems—without the written permission of
the publisher.

Printed in the United States of America
1 2 3 4 5 6 7 07 06 05 04 03

Printer: West

0-534-61698-4

For more information about our products,
contact us at:
Thomson Learning Academic Resource Center
1-800-423-0563

For permission to use material from this text,
contact us by:
Phone: 1-800-730-2214
Fax: 1-800-730-2215
Web: http://www.thomsonrights.com

Wadsworth/Thomson Learning
10 Davis Drive
Belmont, CA 94002-3098
USA

Asia
Thomson Learning
5 Shenton Way #01-01
UIC Building
Singapore 068808

Australia/New Zealand
Thomson Learning
102 Dodds Street
Southbank, Victoria 3006
Australia

Canada
Nelson
1120 Birchmount Road
Toronto, Ontario M1K 5G4
Canada

Europe/Middle East/South Africa
Thomson Learning
High Holborn House
50/51 Bedford Row
London WC1R 4LR
United Kingdom

Latin America
Thomson Learning
Seneca, 53
Colonia Polanco
11560 Mexico D.F.
Mexico

Spain/Portugal
Paraninfo
Calle/Magallanes, 25
28015 Madrid, Spain

TERRORISM:
An Interdisciplinary Perspective
Third Edition
Edited by Thomson Learning/Wadsworth

All material is copyrighted by Thomson Learning/Wadsworth.

Part I: Background to Terrorism

Part I: Components of this section draw upon the expertise of Dr. Jonathan R. White, author of Terrorism: An Introduction, Fourth Edition, 2002 Update *(Wadsworth 2003). White's text is a component of The Wadsworth Contemporary Issues in Crime and Justice Series. The second essay was written by Michael Thomas whose area of expertise includes the study of terrorism. The first essay presents several of the most frequently accepted definitions of terrorism. In subsequent essays, the discussion focuses on transnational terrorism, the origins of Middle Eastern terrorism, and issues relevant to technological and biological acts of terrorism.*

A.   Terrorism Defined

Before introducing the various definitions of terrorism, a word of caution is in order. Although terrorism may be regarded by powerful Western nations such as the United States, as immoral, illegal, and offensive in nature, other nations often consider it an outlet of expression that originates from a deep sense of injustice and oppression by the powerful. Regardless of how the reader feels towards terrorism, it is important to recognize that, in order to understand terrorism as a social phenomenon, we must defy our own way of thinking and consider the perceptions of inequality and oppression held by others towards the United States. Perhaps by achieving a better understanding of the nature of terrorist acts, we will collectively deplore violent resolutions aimed at solving matters of inequality.

There are numerous definitions of terrorism. Some include specific acts that must be present in order to qualify an act as terroristic in nature, while others offer a more general perspective towards the meaning of a terrorism act. The following are classical and contemporary definitions of terrorism. When considered together, they provide accurate, comprehensive and unique dimensions on terrorism.

U.S. State Department and the Central Intelligence Agency (CIA): The U.S. Government has employed the definition of terrorism for statistical and analytical purposes since 1983 as contained in Title 22 of the United States Code, Section 2656f(d). That statute contains the following definitions:

The term "terrorism" means premeditated, politically motivated violence perpetrated against noncombatant (1) targets by subnational groups or clandestine agents, usually intended to influence an audience. The term "international terrorism" means terrorism involving citizens or the territory of more than one country. The term "terrorist group" means any group practicing, or that has significant subgroups that practice, international terrorism.

(1) For purposes of this definition, the term "noncombatant" is interpreted to include, in addition to civilians, military personnel who at the time of the incident are unarmed and/or not on duty.

SOURCE: [http://www.armscontrolcenter.org/terrorism/101/definitions.html]

Federal Bureau of Investigation (FBI): The FBI defines terrorism as ". . .the unlawful use of force or violence against persons or property to intimidate or coerce a government, the civilian population, or any segment thereof, in furtherance of political or social objectives." The FBI further describes terrorism as either domestic or international, depending on the origin, base, and objectives of the terrorist organization. Domestic terrorism is the unlawful use, or threatened use, of force or violence by a group or individual based and operating entirely within the United States or its territories without foreign direction committed against persons or property to intimidate or coerce a government, the civilian population, or any segment thereof, in furtherance of political or social objectives. International terrorism involves violent acts dangerous to human life that are a violation of the criminal laws of the United States or any state, or that would be a criminal violation if committed within the jurisdiction of the United States or any state. These acts appear to be intended to intimidate or coerce a civilian population, influence the policy of a government by intimidation or coercion, or affect the conduct of a government by assassination or kidnapping. International terrorist acts occur outside the United States or transcend national boundaries in terms of the means by which they are accomplished, the persons they appear intended to coerce or intimidate, or the locale in which the perpetrations operate or seek asylum.

SOURCES: [http://www.fbi.gov/publications/terror/terror99.pdf]
and [http://www.terrorismfiles.org/encyclopaedia/terrorism.html]

Vice President's Task Force, 1986: Terrorism is the unlawful use or threat of violence against persons or property to further political or social objectives. It is usually intended to intimidate or coerce a government, individuals or groups, or to modify their behavior or politics.

SOURCE: [http://www.geocities.com/CapitolHill/2468/def.html]

United Nations: In the *International Convention for the Suppression of the Financing of Terrorism,* which entered into force on April 10, 2002, the UN defines terrorism as any . . . act intended to cause death or serious bodily injury to a civilian, or to any other person not taking an active part in the hostilities in a situation of armed conflict, when the purpose of such act, by its nature or context, is to intimidate a population, or to compel a government or an international organization to do or to abstain from doing any act.

SOURCE: [http://www.armscontrolcenter.org/terrorism/101/definitions.html]

U.S. Department of Defense: Terrorism is the calculated use of unlawful violence or threat of unlawful violence to inculcate fear; intended to coerce or to intimidate governments or societies in the pursuit of goals that are generally political, religious, or ideological.

SOURCE: [http://www.armscontrolcenter.org/terrorism/101/definitions.html]

President George W. Bush, Executive Order 13224 on Terrorist Financing: The term "terrorism" means an activity that (i) involves a violent act or an act dangerous to human life, property, or infrastructure; and (ii) appears to be intended (A) to intimidate or coerce a civilian population; (B) to influence the policy of a government by intimidation or coercion; or (C) to affect the conduct of a government by mass destruction, assassination, kidnapping, or hostage-taking.

SOURCE: [http://www.whitehouse.gov/news/releases/2001/09/20010924-1.html]

B. Addressing, Classifying, and Designating Transnational Terrorism
This essay was exclusively written for this publication by Michael Thomas, The University of Texas at Arlington.

Governmental responses to transnational terrorism are manifested in forms ranging from apparently taking no retaliatory action whatsoever, to economic sanctions and trade restrictions placed against nations and other entities harboring or supporting transnational terrorist organizations. At times, governmental responses and retaliatory actions have even included overt or covert military action against such nations or transnational terrorist groups.

It is difficult to pinpoint an exact or commonly accepted definition of transnational terrorism. It can be thought of, however, as terrorist attacks, incidents or other actions perpetrated by a group or organization against the civilian population or government of a nation other than their own, in furtherance of political or social objectives.

As will be demonstrated, the United States' response to terrorism has taken many forms, but it has overwhelmingly failed at deterring any future attacks. In addition, such reactionary policies enacted by the United States government have also failed to address any underlying issues or fundamental motivations of transnational terrorism.

Some may argue that the United States has, at times, appeared to appropriately respond and even retaliate for most acts of transnational terrorism. However, as will be discussed the vast majority of such United States reactionary policies and actions have failed to diminish, deter or otherwise prevent, future attacks.

This inquiry begins by providing a discussion relevant to the methods by which the United States government categorizes, classifies and designates transnational terrorist groups. This section continues with a brief overview of the immediate response policy currently employed by the federal government towards domestic terrorist attacks, or attacks occurring within the U.S. mainland. In conclusion, policies, actions and retaliations the United States has employed in response to previous incidents of transnational terrorism are discussed.

<u>Classification and Designation of Terrorist Groups</u>

The FBI is the only governmental entity offering any methods or typologies for the categorical classification of terrorist groups or organizations. According to former FBI director Louis Freeh in testimony before the U.S. Senate in May 2001, the transnational terrorist threat can be divided into the three categories: "loosely affiliated extremists," "formal terrorist organizations," and "state-sponsors of terrorism" (Freeh 2001, 2).

Former director Freeh testified that the "loosely affiliated extremists" category included groups or organizations motivated by political or religious beliefs; and moreover, that the single common element among these groups was their commitment to the "radical international jihad movement" (Ibid.). In his testimony, Freeh characterized this movement as embracing a "radicalized" Islamic ideology. This ideology promotes an agenda endorsing the use of violence against the "enemies of Islam" in order to overthrow all governments not ruled by Sharia, or conservative Islamic law (Ibid.). Continuing with his testimony, former director Freeh also advised that a primary tactical objective of terrorist groups in this category was the planning and carrying out of large-scale, high-profile, high-casualty terrorist attacks against U.S. interests and citizens (Ibid.).

Discussing the category of "formal terrorist organizations," Freeh stated that the category was comprised of transnational organizations having their own infrastructures, personnel, financial arrangements, and training facilities (Ibid.). Freeh further commented on how these organizations are capable of implementing transnational terrorist attacks on an international basis, and then added that several groups from the "loosely affiliated extremists" category can also be categorized as "formal terrorist organizations" (Ibid.).

In his testimony, Freeh argued that the category of "state-sponsored terrorism" included countries utilizing transnational terrorism as an instrument of foreign policy (Ibid., 3). In conclusion, he advised that the Department of State listed the seven countries of Iran, Iraq, Sudan, Libya, Syria, Cuba and North Korea as state-sponsors of terrorism (Ibid.).

As evidenced above, the only agency within the federal government to offer any categorical approach to transnational terrorism is the FBI. Although the State Department may not categorize transnational terrorist groups, it is responsible for designating specific foreign terrorist organizations (U.S. Department of State 1999, 1) (U.S. Department of State 2001a and b, p. 1). Pursuant to the Antiterrorism and Effective Death Penalty Act of 1996, the office of the Secretary of State is responsible for determining what groups and organizations shall be designated foreign terrorist organizations, hereafter referred to as FTO (Ibid.). Any group so designated by the Secretary of State will remain on the Foreign Terrorist Organization list for two years, at the end of which the group must be re-designated as an FTO or be subject to a mandatory removal from the list (Ibid.). A re-designation by the Secretary of State is a determination that the organization is continuing to engage in and remains supportive of terrorist activity (Ibid.).

Criteria for designation as an FTO include that the entity is a foreign organization, engaging in terrorist activity as defined by appropriate Federal statute, and its activities must threaten the security of United States nationals, or threaten the national security of the United States (Ibid.). The effects of an FTO designation make it unlawful for a person in the United States, or subject to the jurisdiction of the United States, to provide funds or other material support to designated organizations (Ibid.). Also, representatives of FTO's are unable to gain entry to the United States. In addition, financial institutions in the United States must block any organizational funds and report the blockage of these to the appropriate federal agency (Ibid.). Other contributory effects of a designation include a heightened sense of public awareness and scrutiny concerning terrorist organizations, the deterrence of international donations or support for such organizations, and the isolation of an FTO before the international community (Ibid.).

As of May 2003, thirty-six groups have been designated as foreign terrorist organizations. In October 2001, Secretary of State Colin Powell redesignated 25 of the 28 FTOs whose designations were due to expire, combining two previously designated groups (Kahane Chai and Kach) into one. Secretary Powell then designated eight additional FTOs between October 2001 and May 2003.

A Historical Review of Governmental Responses to Transnational Terrorism

Transnational terrorists may choose from a multitude of attack methodologies ranging from kidnapping, bombing, hijacking, assassination and other such methods and tactics. Equally, there exists a vast array of probable and likely responses governments may implement when formalizing their reaction to such incidents. Ultimately, perpetrators of transnational terrorist attacks hold the advantage over any governmental response, as they know when, where and how they will strike. Consequently, governmental first responders are often relegated to a position of lying in wait before initiating any form of viable response.

The United States first faced a transnational terrorist incident on May 1, 1961, when Puerto Rican born Antuillo Ortiz hijacked a National Airlines flight at gunpoint, and ordered it to Cuba where he was granted asylum (U.S. Department of State 2001, 1). Ortiz's hijacking sparked a chain reaction of events culminating in the first of many governmental responses to terrorism. In that particular case, Ortiz's hijacking led to the development and creation of the sky marshals program. The program secretly placed armed federal officers on civilian airliners throughout the United States in hope of preventing any attempted hijacking or air piracy. As a direct result of the terrorist attacks on September 11, 2001, the sky marshals program has been significantly expanded in both size and responsibility. Both of these program expansions are examples of likely responses from the United States government when dealing with acts of terrorism.

The 1979 takeover of the United States Embassy in Tehran, Iran was the next significant transnational terrorist attack demanding a response from the United States government (Ibid.). The Iranian Hostage Crisis began when President Carter admitted the exiled Shah of Iran into the United States for medical treatment in November 1979. In outrage, Iranian students loyal to the Ayatollah laid siege to the U.S. embassy in Tehran, and in the process captured sixty-six Americans. The students initially released thirteen hostages but held the remaining fifty-three for more than a year (Simonsen and Spindlove 2000, 34).

The Carter administration immediately began negotiations with Khomeini's regime, but was unsuccessful in gaining the hostages' release. Eventually President Carter ordered a secret military operation to rescue the hostages by force. However, the military operation failed when a helicopter collided with a transport plane killing several American servicemen in the Iranian desert outside of Tehran. Upon learning of the deadly collision, President Carter immediately aborted the rescue operation and resumed a strategy of negotiation with the Khomeini regime. The hostages were eventually released once his administration ended with the inauguration of Ronald Reagan on January 20, 1981 (U.S. Department of State 2001, 2).

During the 1980s, the United States was faced with a series of transnational terrorist attacks against tourists, civilian and military personnel, overseas military installations, embassies, consulates and other official establishments (U.S. Department of State 2001, 1-11). These attacks have been manifested in the form of hijackings, assassinations, kidnappings, bombings, shootings and other likely modes of attack (Ibid.). The United States has utilized retaliatory responses ranging from taking no apparent retaliatory action, freezing financial assets of culpable groups and organizations, and diplomatic efforts aimed at curbing future attacks, to the use of quick decisive military action such as bombing raids or other direct military action.

For example, in 1986 when a Libyan bomb exploded in a Berlin disco killing two and injuring seventy-six American servicemen, the United States responded with the heavy bombing of several Libyan cities (Ibid., 2) (Jentleson 1991, 63). Proponents of the United States retaliatory bombing cite it as an accurate and appropriate deterrent response resulting in a reduction of Libyan state-sponsored transnational terrorism. However, critics of the retaliatory bombing claim it served no deterrent effect and only acted as motivation for the subsequent Libyan bombing of Pam Am flight 103 over Lockerbie, Scotland in December 1988 (U.S. Department of State 2001, 4) (Simonsen and Spindlove 2000, 50).

Throughout the early and mid 1980s Beirut, Lebanon was a city divided between warring factions. As a result and in order to reaffirm the Lebanese government's control of the area, President Reagan ordered two subsequent contingents of U.S. Marines into Beirut to act as peacekeepers in support of the Lebanese Army (Jentleson 1991, 65-66). The first contingent of

Marines successfully accomplished the stated mission objectives ahead of schedule and withdrew from the area.

Fighting amongst the warring factions ensued several months later, and the Marines were ordered back into Beirut (Ibid.). With this second deployment, Jentleson suggested the U.S. strategy had shifted from one of deterrence to one of coercive diplomacy. This policy shift can be noted in the fact that the Marines were now directly supporting the Lebanese Army with artillery and naval gunfire; as opposed to their first deployment when the Marines served only as a show of force to the warring factions (Ibid.).

In retaliation against the United States for their second intervention in Beirut, the American embassy was bombed on April 18, 1983 by the transnational terrorist group Islamic Jihad (U.S. Department of State 2001, 2). In response to this suicide bombing, the White House ordered the Marines to respond with sustained heavy artillery, naval gunfire and aerial bombardments of areas known to be in control on the Islamic Jihad. This response, in the eyes of American officials, appeared adequate due to the reduction of sniper attacks initiated on Marine positions, and the reduced resistance experienced during several combat patrols conducted throughout the city.

However, this retaliatory response did not deter future actions by Islamic Jihad because on October 23, 1983, a suicide bomber detonated a 12,000-pound truck bomb at Marine headquarters killing 242 Marines and wounding hundreds of others (Ibid.) (Jentleson 1991, 66). The United States government responded to this transnational terrorist attack with no apparent retaliatory action. The Reagan administration ordered the Marines to withdraw from Beirut.

Shortly after the Marines left Beirut in late 1983, transnational terrorist groups began kidnapping and assassinating foreign nationals from the United States and Great Britain. In response to these murders and kidnappings, the United States refused to negotiate with the responsible parties, choosing rather to depend solely upon diplomatic efforts in gaining the hostages' release (Ibid.) (Simonsen and Spindlove 2000, 151). While the White House refused to negotiate, eighteen American citizens were kidnapped and held hostage between 1984 and 1986 (Jentleson 1991, 66).

The common characteristic of the aforementioned attacks is that all were perpetrated overseas, and not a single transnational terrorist attack had ever occurred in the United States (Ibid., 1-4). That is, until the World Trade Center was the target of transnational terrorists' truck bomb on February 26, 1993. The bombing was the first transnational terrorist attack ever to occur in the United States (mainland).

The resulting explosion left six people dead and over 1,000 injured. Local and state emergency personnel quickly arrived on scene, controlled the resulting fire and treated anyone injured in the blast. The FBI opened a criminal investigation, and identified, arrested and convicted the terrorists involved in this incident.

On the morning of April 19, 1995, the Murrah Federal Building in Oklahoma City, Oklahoma was destroyed by a truck bomb (Ibid., 5) killing 168 people. As in the case of the World Trade Center bombing in 1993, the United States government had no firm or official policies, procedures for the local, state and federal agencies responding to the terror incident.

In fact, the only federal document or publication applicable to the situation was *The Federal Response Plan,* a 1992 Federal Emergency Management Administration publication detailing how the federal government would coordinate with local and state agencies in the event of natural disasters (Federal Emergency Management Administration 1999, 1).

This lack of federal guidance and oversight resulted in the creation of many policies and procedures eventually adopted by the federal government for use by local, state and federal agencies when responding to a terrorist incident. The evolution of these official federal governmental policies, procedures and publications will now be briefly discussed.

As previously mentioned, when terrorist attacks occurred at the World Trade Center in 1993 and at the Murrah Federal Building in Oklahoma City in 1995, there was a clear absence of federal publications, guidelines, policies or procedures advising local, state and federal agencies on how to respond or collaborate. The first official document addressing this gaping lapse in governmental oversight was Presidential Directive 39, or PDD-39, released by President Bill Clinton on June 21, 1995 (Clinton 1995, 1). PDD-39 was later followed by the *Terrorism Annex* of *The Federal Response Plan* in April of 1999, and the *United States Government Interagency Domestic Terrorism Concept of Operations Plan*, commonly known as CONPLAN, in January 2001 (U.S. Department of Defense et al., 2001, 2). These publications set forth the United States government's official reactionary policies and procedures regarding any domestic terrorist incident, and served to address the previous lapse in federal guidance discovered following the 1993 World Trade Center and 1995 Oklahoma City terrorist attacks.

Although the United States government had appeared to adequately address the domestic response to terrorist attacks, the governmental response to incidents of transnational terrorism still failed to deter or prevent ongoing attacks. September 13, 1995, a rocket-propelled grenade was directed at the United States Embassy in Moscow (U.S. Department of State 2001, 5). The attack was in retaliation for U.S. military air strikes against Serbian artillery positions in Bosnia. The Clinton administration chose no overt retaliation or response to the Moscow embassy incident (Ibid.).

A similar rocket attack against the United States Embassy in Athens took place on February 15, 1996, with members of the 17 November group claiming responsibility. Again, no retaliatory response was taken (Ibid., 6). It can be inferred that the lack of response to the Moscow incident might have led directly to the 17 November group's decision to attack the Athens embassy.

On June 25, 1996, a fuel truck carrying a bomb exploded outside a U.S. military barracks in Saudi Arabia known as Khobar Towers, killing nineteen servicemen and injuring 515 people (Ibid.). Several transnational terrorist groups claimed responsibility; however, evidence later revealed a strong connection to terrorists associated with Usama Bin Laden. Just as with the two embassy attacks, the Clinton administration chose no retaliatory action, and suggested the Khobar Towers bombing was an isolated incident and not likely to be repeated in the future.

However, on August 7, 1998 the U.S. embassies in Nairobi, Kenya and Dar er Salaam, Tanzania were simultaneously bombed causing the combined deaths of eighteen United States citizens and injuring more than 5,500 persons (Ibid., 8). Usama Bin Laden was held responsible for both transnational terrorist attacks. The US responded with retaliatory strikes of cruise missiles in Sudan and aerial bombing raids in Afghanistan against camps financed and operated by Bin Laden. At the time, the Clinton administration believed the retaliatory action to be appropriate and effective, much like the Reagan administration believed their actions in Beirut to be effective and adequate.

The retaliatory action was again proven unable to deter future transnational terrorist attacks by Usama Bin Laden, when October 12, 2000, the USS Cole was attacked in the port of Aden, Yemen (Ibid., 10). Bin Laden was found to have financed and supported the transnational terrorists who had rammed the USS Cole with a small dinghy filled with explosives (Ibid.). In retaliation, the Clinton administration again ordered the aerial bombardment of camps in Afghanistan owned, operated and financed by Usama Bin Laden.

Finally, on September 11, 2001, at roughly 8:45 A.M. an American Airlines jet flew into one of the World Trade Center towers. Early reports cited pilot error or an obvious mechanical failure; that is, until eighteen minutes later when a worldwide cable news audience witnessed a second jetliner slam into the remaining World Trade Center tower. The tragedy continued with reports that a third airliner had crashed into the Pentagon, and that a forth and final aircraft had plummeted nose first into a barren field in rural Pennsylvania.

All told, more than 3,000 Americans and some 500 citizens from over 90 different countries died in the worst terrorist attack in history. In repudiated disbelief, the American public faced the painful truth that transnational terrorists had perpetrated the most deadly terrorist attack in American history, not on some distant foreign shore, but in the mainland of the United States of America.[1]

Works Cited

Brophy-Baermann,Bryan, and Conybaere, John A. C. 1994. Retaliating against
    Terrorism: Rational Expectations and the Optimality of Rules versus Discretion.
    American Journal of Political Science 38, no. 1:196-210.

Clinton, William J. President of the United States. 1995. Presidential Decision
    Directive 39. Washington, D.C.

Enders, Walter, Sander, Todd, and Cauley, John. 1990. UN Conventions, Technology,
    and Retaliation in the Fight against Terrorism. *Terrorism and Political Violence 77*, no.
    2:84-105.

Enders, Walter and Sandler, Todd. 1993. The Effectiveness of Antiterrorism
    Policies: A Vector-Autoregression-Intervention Analysis. *The American Political Science
    Review* 87, no. 4:829-844.

Enders, Walter and Sandler, Todd. 2000. Is Transnational Terrorism Becoming More
    Threatening? *Journal of Conflict Resolution* 44, no. 3:307-33.

Federal Emergency Management Agency. 1999a. *Federal Response Plan.*
    Washington, D.C.

Federal Emergency Administration Agency. 1999b. Terrorism Incident Annex.
    Washington, D.C.

Freeh, Louis. Director Federal Bureau of Investigations. 2001. *Threat of Terrorism
    to the United States.* Washington, D.C.

Jentleson, Bruce W. 1991. The Reagan Administration and Coercive Diplomacy: Restraining More Than Remaking Governments. *Political Science Quarterly* 106, no. 1: 57-82.

Sandler, Todd, Tschirhart, John T., and Cauley, John. 1983. A Theoretical Analysis of Transnational Terrorism. *The American Political Science Review* 77, no. 1:36-54.

Simonsen, Clifford E., and Spindlove, Jeremy R. 2000. *Terrorism today: the past, the players and the future*. Upper Saddle River, New Jersey: Prentice-Hall.

U.S. Departments of Defense. U.S. Department of Energy. U.S. Department of Health and Human Services. U.S. Department of Justice. Federal Bureau of Investigation. Environmental Protection Agency. Federal Emergency Management Administration. 2001. *CONPLAN: United States Government Interagency Domestic Terrorism Concept of Operations Plan*. Washington, D.C.

U.S. Department of State. Office of the Coordinator for Counterterrorism. 1999. *Designations by Secretary of State Madeline K. Albright*. Washington, D.C.

U.S. Department of State. Office of the Historian. 2001a. *Significant Terrorist Incidents, 1961-2001*. Washington, D.C.

U.S. Department of State. Office of the Coordinator for Counterterrorism. 2001b. *2001 Report on Foreign Terrorist Organizations*. Washington, D.C.

[1] For a detailed discussion, description and presentation of suggested models of governmental response and terrorist classification refer to Michael Thomas (2002). *"Transnational Terrorism and Terrorist Design: Modalities of Organizational Structure and Problem-Solving Proposed."* Thesis abstracts, The University of Texas at Arlington. Department of Criminology and Criminal Justice.

D. Origins of Middle Eastern Terrorism

The excerpt was written by Jonathan R. White, Terrorism: An Introduction, Fourth Edition, 2002 Update (Wadsworth, 2003)

The origins of modern terrorism have been reviewed in terms of its spread from Western European ideology to Russia, then back to the West by the incorporation of Russian revolutionary thought in the nationalist struggle in Ireland. Before discussing modern terrorism, it is necessary to look at the historical development of conflict in the Middle East. Several Middle Eastern groups took the concepts of modern terrorism and transformed them into a mode of conflict. This chapter introduces the development of religious and historical conflicts in the Middle East and the historical role of terrorism in the area.

An Introduction to the Region

The term Middle East refers to a section of the world that encompasses North Africa, Southwest Asia directly south of Turkey including the Arabian Peninsula, Iran, and Afghanistan. (See map in Figure 1.) Some commentators also include Pakistan in their geographical definition of Middle East because it is dominated by Islamic culture. The term was coined by American naval strategist Alfred Thayer Mahan toward the end of the nineteenth century. Albert Hourani (1997) presents one of the most definitive histories of the area. According to Hourani, the area is dominated by two major concerns: the religion of Islam and the history of the Arab people.

The Prophet Mohammed, the founder of Islam, received a series of revelations from Gabriel, an angel known in Hebrew and Christian traditions, about 610 C.E. Mystified by his encounters with the angel and unable to write, Mohammed returned to his family after each event and related the angel's accounts of God's desires for humanity in a series of poems and verses. Dutiful family members recorded these revelations, and they were incorporated into a holy book called the Q'ran, or the Verses. Mohammed, elated by his angelic encounters with the Almighty, spread a message of universalism, love, and monotheism.

Although Mohammed's message was essentially based on love, discipline, and submission to God's will, merchants in his hometown of Mecca were incensed by his religious pronouncements. Mohammed spoke of a final judgment against evil. Such eschatology threatened the religious trade of Mecca, a trade center where various cultures crossed paths and many deities flourished in an atmosphere of polytheism. In short, there was a profit to be made in statues, charms, and relics, and Mohammed's talk of one universal power uniting humankind was bad for business. The merchants took the only logical step they could see. They tried to kill Mohammed.

Fleeing from Mecca, the Prophet's utterances did not stop. He gained a large following and in a few years returned to Mecca not only with a message of love, but also with a sword. Mohammed declared a holy war, a jihad, on all nonbelievers. Mecca became a holy city, and the Arab realm of Islam spread. At the time of his death about 632, Islam was a dominating and growing force in the Middle East.

Mohammed's followers spread Islam and Arabic culture through the Middle East in the years after his death. Two dynasties of leaders, the Umayyads (661–750) and the Abbasids (750–1258), ruled the area in the years following Mohammed. Hourani points out that these leaders, or caliphs, theologically divided the world into the Realm of Islam and the Realm of War. The purpose of Islam was to subject the world to God's will. Indeed, *Islam* means submission to the will of God, and a *Muslim* is one who submits.

About 1000 C.E. the Turks began to take the domains of the Abbasids. Struggles continued for the next 100 years until a Mongol advance from East Asia brought the Abbasid dynasty to an end. The Mongols were eventually stopped by an Egyptian army of slaves, and their descendants gave rise to a new group of Turks known as Ottomans. The Ottomans were aggressive, conquering most of the Middle East and large parts of Europe. The Ottomans fought the Iranians on one border and central Europeans on the other border for many years.

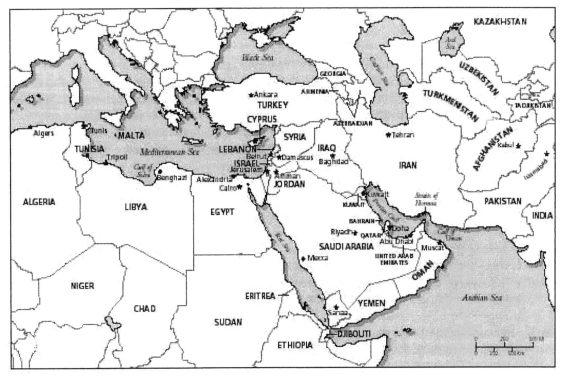

Figure 1 Map of the Middle East

European relations with Islamic empires were not characterized by harmony. The West began its first violent encounters with the European attempts to conquer the Middle East known as the Crusades (1095 to about 1250). These affairs were bloody and instigated centuries of hatred and distrust between Muslims and Christians. European struggles with the Ottoman Empire reinforced years of military tensions between the two civilizations. Modern tensions in the area can be traced to the decline of Ottoman influence and the collapse of Iranian power in the eighteenth century. When these Islamic powers receded, Western Christian powers were quick to fill the void.

Yonah Alexander (1976) points out that issues of power shifts were complicated by a late nineteenth century concept called Zionism. Zionists began moving to Palestine in the 1890s for the purpose of establishing a Jewish homeland. This created some tension, as Syria and Egypt were vying for control of the area. The problem exploded in 1914, when World War I internationalized the political problems of the Middle East. Modern Middle Eastern terrorism can be traced to World War I's (1914–1918) political watershed.

A Synopsis of Some Major Problems

To understand terrorism in the Middle East, it is necessary to appreciate certain recent aspects of the region's history. To best understand the Middle East, keep the following assumptions in mind:
1.   The current structure of Middle Eastern geography and political rule is a direct result of nineteenth century European imperial influence in the region and the outcomes of World War I.
2.   Many of the Arab countries in the Middle East place more emphasis on the power of the family than on contemporary notions of government. However, Israel rules itself as a parliamentary democracy.

3. The modern state of Israel is not the nation mentioned in the Hebrew and Christian Bibles or the Islamic Q'ran. It is a secular power dominated by people of European descent.

4. Arabs, and Palestinians in particular, do not hold a monopoly on terrorism.

5. The religious differences in the region have developed over centuries, and fanaticism in any one of them can spawn violence. There are fanatical Jews, Christians, and Muslims in the Middle East who practice terrorism in the name of religion.

6. Although the Middle East has been volatile since 1948, the year Israel was recognized as a nation-state, modern terrorism grew after 1967. It increased after 1973 and became a standard method of military operations in the following two decades.

7. In 1993, however, the Palestine Liberation Organization (PLO) renounced terrorism. Ironically, this has created tremendous tension. On the Arab side, some groups have denounced the PLO's actions while others have embraced it. The same reaction has occurred in Israel, where one set of political parties endorses peace plans and another prepares for war. Middle Eastern peace is a very fragile process, and terrorism is a wild card. It can upset delicate negotiations at any time, even after a peace treaty has been signed and implemented (for an example, see Hoffman, 1995).

8. All of these issues are complicated by a shortage of water and vast differences in social structure. The area contains some of the world's richest and some of the world's poorest people. Most of them are far from water sources.

One can best begin to understand the Middle East by focusing on the world of the late 1800s. During that time period, three critical events took place that helped to shape the modern Middle East.

First, the Ottoman Empire, the Turk-based government that ruled much of the Middle East, was falling apart in the nineteenth century. This meant the Ottoman Turks encountered domestic challenges across their empire as various nationalistic, tribal, and familial groups revolted, and they faced foreign threats, too. The Iranian empire had collapsed earlier, but Great Britain, France, Germany, and Russia intervened in the area with military force. Each European country was willing to promise potential rebels many things, if they revolted against the Turks. Realistically, few of those promises could be kept.

The second critical event came from a political movement called Zionism. From 1896 to 1906, European Jews, separated from their ancient homeland for nearly 2,000 years, wanted to create their own nation. Some of them favored Palestine, whereas others wanted to move to Argentina. In 1906, those who backed Palestine won the argument, and European Jews increasingly moved to the area. They did not ask the Palestinian Arabs, the people who lived in Palestine, for permission.

Finally, European armies engulfed the Middle East from 1914 to 1918, as they fought World War I. They continued to make contradictory promises as they sought to gain spheres of influence in the region. When the war ended, the victorious nations felt they had won the area from the Turks. They divided the Middle East, not with respect to future political problems but to share the spoils of victory. This created long-term political problems.

<u>Three Sources of Middle Eastern Terrorism</u>

The situation at the end of World War I set the stage for developments over the next 80 years. The political situation gave rise to three sources of terrorism in the Middle East: (1) questions about the political control of Palestine, (2) questions of who would rule the Arab world, and (3) questions concerning the relations between the two main branches of Islam: Sunnis and Shiites. Stated another way, these problems are:

1.   The Palestinian question (control of Palestine)
2.   Intra-Arab rivalries/struggles
3.   The Iranian Revolution

These problems are all separate, but they are also interrelated. The sources of terrorism in the Middle East are symbiotic. That is, they are independent arenas of violence with a dynamic force of their own, but they are also related to and dependent on each other.

All forms of Middle Eastern terrorism exhibit certain common traits. Primarily, many Arab groups express dissatisfaction over the existence of Israel. They are not necessarily pro-Palestinian, but they find the notion of a European-created, non-Arab state in their lands offensive. Most Middle Eastern terrorist groups are anti-imperialist. The intensity of their passion wavers according to the type of group, but terrorism has largely been dominated by anti-Western feelings. Another symbiotic factor is the pan-Arabic or pan-Islamic orientation of terrorist groups. Although they fight for local control, most wish to revive a united Arab realm of Islam. Finally, Middle Eastern terrorism is united by kinship bonds. In terrorism, as in Middle Eastern politics in general, familial links are often more important than national identification.

D. Technological, Nuclear, Biological and Chemical Terrorism, and Cyberterrorism
The excerpt derives from Jonathan R. White, Terrorism: An Introduction, Fourth Edition, 2002 Update (Wadsworth, 2003).

<u>U.S. Vulnerability to Technological Terrorism</u>

The United States is the most technologically advanced superpower in the world. Technology has opened new doors to the future, which many Americans have taken for granted. Other national competitors have taken advantage of the United States's nonchalant attitude toward technology at times, but the United States stands as one of the masters of new industrial and technological techniques. Along with Japan and Western Europe, the United States is a technologically oriented society.

The irony of U.S. success with technology is that the country has become vulnerable to attacks on technology and by technology. One does not have to agree with Brian Clark's political position to understand that the United States is dependent on technology (Clark claims that political terrorism will emerge as the foremost problem in the world when terrorists begin to take advantage of technology.) While the military has taken precautions to shield defense and weapons systems from interference, civilian industry has fallen behind. Given U.S. dependence on technology, this has created a window of opportunity for terrorists.

There is no clear way to react to the problem of technological vulnerability. Some analysts, like Halstead and Ballard (1997), have called for rigid new safeguards and massive new security efforts. Others believe a calm assessment of potential threats is more in order (Heim, 1984).

Analysts do not agree about the extent of the threat, and most of them focus on weapons of mass destruction. A study by B. J. Berkowitz et al. (1972) was one of the first to examine the implications of mass destruction weapons in the hands of terrorists. Its conclusion was that civil chaos would result. According to the study, several attempts were made by radical groups to employ some level of chemical and biological weapons (CBW) attack from 1967 to 1970. Although this information is dated, the Aum Shinrikyo attack in Tokyo demonstrates the reality of the threat.

The Berkowitz study points to several areas of vulnerability. Metropolitan water supplies are subject to contamination. Although poisons would dissipate in a large volume of water, general public reaction would be one of panic. In addition, criminal organizations have attempted to produce chemical weapons for extortion and assassination. Berkowitz and his colleagues also point out attempts to steal or produce CBWs in Europe and the United States.

Robert Mullen (1978) also examines modern society's vulnerability to technological weapons. The capacity for mass destruction is a recent historical development. In the past, killing many people required many people to do the killing. Technology has changed this. Mass destruction terrorism can be inferred from CBWs and nuclear weapons.

Mullen states that terrorism based on massively destructive weapons involves skills that few terrorist groups possess. Technical weapons require technical skills and support networks. Many groups lack these capacities, but Mullen says the past may not be indicative of the future. The capability for mass destruction exists.

Robert Kupperman and Darrell Trent (1979) deal with some of the issues posed by technological threats. Kupperman (1985b) examines the issue again, with a specific focus on organizational responses to technological threats, and he describes the potential threat that technological terrorism poses for the United States. Both Kupperman and Trent strike a middle ground, however, between complacently ignoring the problem and overreacting to it.

In Kupperman and Trent's analysis, responsible policies should be developed to meet the potential threat. The response should be one of policy analysis and application. Industrial and technological safeguards will work only if they are accompanied by proper emergency procedures. Kupperman and Trent suggest models for restructuring U.S. federal bureaus and emergency planning networks.

Unlike many analysts, Kupperman and Trent believe the analytical literature on terrorism to be fairly complete. They do not see the need to add to the theoretical body of knowledge. Instead, they argue that Walter Laqueur has appropriately described the historical and social background of terrorism and that Brian Jenkins has adequately analyzed current and future trends. The only gap in the literature is in the area of technology.

The authors were trying to get policy moving in the direction of counterterrorism; technology provided their motivation for writing. Kupperman and Trent believe the problem of technological terrorism has generally been ignored and the U.S. government is woefully underprepared to deal with a technological threat. Accordingly, they describe several horrifying potential scenarios for terrorism (without giving terrorists clues on weapons construction or utilization). They hope the devastating nature of the scenarios will grab policymakers' attention.

Kupperman and Trent believe that social deterrents are insufficient to rule out the use of mass destruction weapons. Increased possession of nuclear and chemical weapons has been accompanied by their use or threatened use. Nation-states have legitimized the use of mass destruction weapons, hence paving the way for terrorists to adopt them. The analysts conclude that it is time to start realizing the truly destructive nature of such weapons.

The most common type of terrorist weapon is a bomb. It has been historically popular, it is easy to deliver, and it poses a difficult puzzle for police to solve. Kupperman and Trent say that when groups mature, they move toward more sophisticated weaponry, but in their initial stages, groups find that bombs are cheap and effective tools. Kupperman and Trent state that the danger is an enhancement of bombs through CBWs or nuclear capacities. Recent experience demonstrates that even sophisticated conventional bombs can destroy civilian aircraft.

Kupperman and Trent argue either type of weapon can be used for psychological impact, and they predict the public would react with panic if either nuclear or CBW agents were introduced by terrorists. They believe that because nuclear bombs are difficult to make or steal, terrorists would achieve the same psychological impact by spreading radioactive materials. If accompanied by an effective means to spread the toxins, chemical and biological weapons have a similar potential.

Attacks on technological targets are another way to achieve mass destruction without the need for technological weapons. In addition, Kupperman and Trent point to the ability of terrorists to paralyze the economy by attacking targets necessary for production and service. Electrical power grids are important from this standpoint, and the most likely targets are transmission lines and transformers. Gas and petroleum lines are even more vulnerable, and conventional and nuclear power plants present tempting targets. They also consider the vulnerability of computer networks.

In Kupperman and Trent's analysis, counterterrorism must begin with a reorganization of the federal bureaucracy. Without discussing the specifics for each agency, their recommendations can be summarized in two steps. First, the analysts want a few key federal agencies to have definite responsibility for emergency situations. The role of individual agencies should be spelled out in policy guidelines, and bureaucratic managers should be held responsible for their agencies' abilities to deal with potential terrorism.

In their second series of recommendations, Kupperman and Trent want the government to develop realistic management plans to coordinate the response of its various units. There is a need to develop a small, knowledgeable crisis staff to direct operations in the event of a technological attack. According to the researchers, it is not necessary to become preoccupied with the counterterrorist functions of each agency because mass destruction terrorism is a low probability occurrence. However, preparing for an event with key managers can serve as both a deterrent and a practical method to restore normalcy in the event of an attack.

Some security specialists have focused on the idea of prevention. Indeed, it comprises the philosophy of such organizations as the American Society for Industrial Security. Prevention of technological terrorism is a corollary to safeguarding technological materials. Robert Kindilien (1985) makes this argument with reference to the nuclear power industry. Enhanced security will reduce the risk of losing dangerous material and waste. American industry is currently vulnerable to such losses. Kindilien says it is necessary to assess risks and attack them with an aggressive security system.

Another point about the vulnerability of the United States has been raised by many analysts. If a mass destruction threat developed, the initial public reaction would probably be one of panic. A fear of chemical weapons and radioactivity pervades popular culture. If the American public believed a major city was in jeopardy, there is reason to believe fear would sweep the nation. In a climate of fear, cherished liberties can be destroyed.

Russell Ayers (1975) and John Barton (1980) have raised this issue. In this sense, the corollary to technological terrorism is another threat. In reacting to potential mass destruction, security and police powers would be increased. In many societies, this has been closely correlated with a decline in civil liberties. The ideal function of the American justice system is to protect individual rights, but historically, in times of panic, the government and the police have forgotten this. There is good reason to believe that technological terrorism would create panic, and civil rights often fall by the wayside in such situations.

Another potential target of technology and terrorism is the energy industry. Oil and gas are the United States's chief means of energy. An article placed in an addendum to the Kupperman and Trent analysis raises the problem of securing the energy industry. The analysis claims the transportation and storage of fossil fuels is not as safe as people tend to assume.

Security Problems in the Energy Industry

The United States relies on energy to support its technology, and the interruption of energy supplies could be construed as a national security threat. If a nation or terrorist group could shut off U.S. energy, it could close down major portions of the economy. Secure energy production, transportation, and storage are all critical to the United States.

Kupperman and Trent state that electrical systems are quite vulnerable. Attacks on key power transformers could stop the flow of electricity to large segments of the country for quite some time. Damage to key generating facilities would also have long-term effects. Currently, the threat is localized. Power stations and transformers have been subject to industrial sabotage, but this has had only local, short-term effects.

Maynard Stephens (1979, pp. 220–223) assesses the vulnerability of U.S. oil and natural gas systems. Stephens argues the interruption of oil and gas delivery would have the most devastating economic impact of any attack on energy. The reason is that oil and gas form the United States' greatest source of energy. Seventy-five percent of U.S. energy needs are filled by oil and gas. Although electrical power grids have backup supplies, no method of continuing service is available if oil and gas lines are destroyed.

According to Stephens, the efficiency of the systems is the major problem. Industry and government planners designed U.S. pipelines for maximum flow and distribution of the product. As a result, oil and gas are channeled over hundreds of miles in a highly efficient and concentrated set of pipelines. But this very efficiency has weakened the security of the system: An attack on a major line would magnify the scope of the attack.

Stephens's main worry is the lack of federal and state concern about protecting the gas and petroleum industries. He claims the government has taken almost no protective measures. Stephens says because domestic terrorism in the United States has not often been manifested, threats to the oil and gas industries appear to be abstract.

Things have changed since Stephens's article appeared. Not only has the United States been subject to domestic terrorism, but also some of it has been supported by foreign governments. Kupperman and Trent appear to have been correct. In the early stages—the World Trade Center and Oklahoma City, for example—the primary weapon has been the bomb. More sophisticated attacks can be expected in the future. The oil and gas distribution systems are perfect targets. Transportation centers and parts are next in line.

To illustrate the point, consider a situation like the 1991 Persian Gulf War. American heavy equipment for the war was shipped through ports along the Atlantic seaboard and the Gulf of Mexico. Assume you are a Middle Eastern leader and the United States is preparing a Desert Storm–style operation against your country. You do not have conventional military forces cable of stopping the United States, but you have several terrorist training camps in your country and links to international terrorist structures inside the United States. What could you do?

If you had the technological sophistication, it would be relatively easy to strike the United States. If you could cause sufficient explosions in the ports at Houston, Charleston, Norfolk, and New York, you would limit American capacity to move heavy equipment to the Middle East. If this was combined with attacks on the electrical power grid and gas pipelines, your efforts would be more effective. Finally, a few well-placed bombs like that in Oklahoma City would cause general panic.

This hypothetical scenario is not designed to make you paranoid, and if it did happen, it probably would not end with a devastating defeat of the United States. In addition, any nation that would attempt such an undertaking would require extensive planning and coordination, something far beyond the leadership capacity of a street thug like Saddam Hussein. If it did happen, however, it would isolate military forces in the region and hamper their supply lines. In the opening stages of Desert Storm, it could have resulted in thousands of American casualties. Therefore, policies and emergency plans must begin to anticipate U.S. technological vulnerability. If terrorism is approached as a legal problem, a national defense role for federal, state, and local police agencies must be recognized.

The Threat of Nuclear Terrorism

The most frequently discussed aspect of future terrorism is nuclear attack, and it seems to have a psychological impact far more frightening than other scenarios. This may be due to the widespread fear of nuclear weapons, or to the fact that a greater body of knowledge on the topic is available to the general public. Regardless, it is frequently impossible to discuss the future of terrorism without examining the potential impact of nuclear weapons or radioactive material (Sanz, 1992).

One of many analysts who have addressed the question of nuclear terrorism, B. David (1985) makes four critical points about the issue. First, nuclear terrorism and chemical and biological weapon terrorism are usually discussed together. Second, true nuclear terrorism requires either a difficult production process or the theft of radioactive materials or weapons; CBW agents are easier to produce and obtain. Third, a key to responding to nuclear terrorism is to discern the motivation of a group that might be willing to use weapons of mass destruction. Finally, there are still social sanctions against employing such weapons.

Martha Crenshaw (1977) raises other points. First, Crenshaw is concerned about the proliferation of nuclear materials on an international level. She believes the abundance of nuclear materials increases the likelihood of nuclear terrorism.

More than two decades after Crenshaw's analysis, the nuclear issue still dominates segments of the international agenda. President Clinton signed a United Nations–sponsored antinuclear treaty in 1996, but some nations, such as India, refused to support the ban. The collapse of the Soviet Union also made active nuclear weapons available to terrorist groups.

Crenshaw also expresses concern about the spread of the nuclear power industry. The number of nuclear power plants increases the potential for attacks on power-generating stations and the theft of waste material. Terrorists who lack the ability to build or buy nuclear weapons can simply obtain nuclear waste from a generating station and detonate it. This would produce a ground level "nuclear" blast, complete with fallout.

Brian Jenkins (1975, 1980, 1986, 1987) has approached the question of nuclear terrorism cautiously and provides several answers. He gave his first answer in 1975, admitting that his conjectures were purely speculative. His answer has been slightly revised through the years, but his initial response has been partially validated by nearly three decades of developments in terrorism. Basically, Jenkins says we do not know whether terrorists will use nuclear weapons but we have no reason to assume that they will automatically evolve in that direction.

Jenkins says nuclear terrorism is possible, but he is reluctant to see it as a major threat. He believes terrorists are rational creatures, and nuclear terrorism is irrational. Nuclear weapons would not work in low-level operations, and once the weapons were deactivated, there would be no incentive for governments to continue to honor any negotiated promises. Social restraints tend to make nuclear devices impractical.

However, the possibility of nuclear terrorism cannot be dismissed. Jenkins points out that many Americans believe nuclear terrorism is more likely than a nuclear war. Trends in nuclear-related terrorism have reinforced public beliefs. Jenkins equates attacks on nuclear facilities with nuclear terrorism, and his data indicate that attacks on the nuclear industry and on weapons facilities are declining. Yet attacks continue, accompanied by the general trend toward an increased level of violence. If nuclear terrorism is not inevitable, it is certainly not impossible.

Nuclear terrorism could take a variety of forms. Jenkins says terrorists could attack nuclear facilities and use the entire area as a weapon. They could also simply steal material or ask a ransom for it. Terrorists could fabricate a nuclear hoax, and the ensuing panic might be as dangerous as a threatened explosion. In the simplest case, terrorists could spread radioactive material; in the most complex case, they might detonate a device. More recently, British sources (Ryan, 1996) indicate that the Russian Mafia has attempted to sell live nuclear weapons and supporting technology on the black market. The term nuclear terrorism is used frequently, but for a variety of potential activities.

Several people have commented on Jenkins's position. Paul Leventhal and Yonah Alexander (1986, pp. 33–53) recorded a speech by Jenkins on nuclear terrorism and some experts' reactions to it. One member of the audience, David Mabry of the U.S. Department of State, agreed with Jenkins about the rationalism of terrorists. Mabry said terrorists do not kill for the sake of killing; they have a political motivation for their actions.

Mabry disagrees with Jenkins's assessment of the probability of nuclear terrorism. Given the increasing violence of terrorist groups, the lure of nuclear terrorism is becoming too great. State sponsors of terrorist groups have greater access to nuclear weapons, further increasing the possibility of such terrorism. Mabry was convinced that Iran and Libya would not hesitate to use nuclear weapons in a terrorist incident. Finally, because bombing is the most popular terrorist act, nuclear bombing might simply be viewed as its logical extension.

Yural Ne'eman, a physics professor and former Israeli cabinet minister, also disagreed with Jenkins. He was critical of Jenkins's reluctance to distinguish attacks on nuclear facilities from the use of nuclear materials in terrorism. Ne'eman said they are not the same thing and they certainly are not positively correlated. Therefore, declining rates of attacks on nuclear facilities had no connection with the probability of a use of nuclear material in terrorism.

Ne'eman also believed most terrorism was state-sponsored. Far from the individual groups that Jenkins imagined, Ne'eman saw most terrorists as an extension of national governments. Ne'eman agreed with Mabry that Iran and Libya were prime candidates for the use of nuclear weapons. He also added Iraq to the list and completely dismissed Jenkins's notion that terrorists would be somehow constrained by a sense of morality.

Larry Collins and Dominique Lapierre (1980) wrote a terrorist thriller titled *The Fifth Horseman* that featured fictional state-sponsored technological terrorism. The premise of the book is that Moamar Khadaffy has managed to construct a hydrogen bomb. He places the weapon in New York City by clandestinely shipping it to the United States with a semiautonomous terrorist group. An army of bureaucrats, emergency personnel, and police officers search for the device while Khadaffy negotiates with the U.S. president about Libyan demands. The United States is paralyzed in its response for a variety of diplomatic reasons.

The premise of the novel is exciting, and the book is fun to read. In the real world, however, the scenario poses some problems. If a nation was to sponsor nuclear terrorism against the United States, it would run the risk of full American military reprisal. Mass destruction could obviously be construed as an act of war; American military forces have been deployed for terrorist events of far less significance than a nuclear explosion. This refers back to the policy debate between legality and defense.

The United States has undertaken efforts to prepare for technological terrorism. According to Christopher Dobson and Ronald Payne (1982b, pp. 51–76), an array of federal agencies has joined forces to combat all acts of domestic terrorism. Donald A. DeVito and Lacy Suiter (1987, pp. 416–432), both directors of state emergency planning agencies, suggest that the Federal Emergency Management Agency (FEMA) be used as the clearinghouse for bureaucratic coordination. They say terrorism demands emergency planning. FEMA has taken a leading role in preparing for effective interaction among local, federal, and state governments. It is supported by a variety of federal regulatory bodies and law enforcement agencies.

Biological and Chemical Terrorism

Chemical and biological agents might well be the weapons of choice should terrorists use weapons of mass destruction. FEMA (1998) gives several reasons. First, biological and chemical agents are easier to produce than nuclear weapons or radioactive material. Second, as many as 26 nations appear to have developed chemical weapons, and 12 more nations are seeking to do so. In addition, 10 other nations have biological weapons programs. Finally, chemical and biological agents are easier to transport and utilize than nuclear weapons. Chemical and biological weapons are relatively easy to use, they are available, and they are mobile. Have they become, as some people argue, the poor person's nuclear bomb?

To answer this question, look at the nature of each agent. Ron Purver (1995) offers an outstanding summary of open source information on chemical and biological agents. Purver says biological weapons are based on microorganisms and poisons produced by plants and animals. Most of the weapons terrorists would use have been classified as agents that would produce fever, a plague, or some other type of infectious disease. Some of the agents are extremely lethal, while others would be used to incapacitate people. Purver also says some terrorism analysts fear the development of a genetically engineered disease.

Chemical agents are not as lethal as biological agents, and they are easier to control. The four common types of chemical weapons are: nerve agents, blood agents, choking agents, and blistering agents (see Table 1). Nerve agents enter the body through contaminated food, water, air, or contact with skin. They cause body fluids to flow uncontrollably from openings in the body and induce muscle spasms. In high doses, victims can go into convulsions, and death may come from the evacuation of body fluids within a matter of minutes. Sarin is a common type of nerve weapon. Blood agents are absorbed through breathing and are carried through the body by breathing. They cause lethal damage by reacting with enzymes in the body. Hydrogen cyanide, the gas used in Nazi concentration camps, is a blood agent. Choking chemicals, such as chlorine gas, attack the lungs and prevent people from breathing. These agents cause the walls of the lungs to flood with mucus, and the victim literally drowns in the secretions. Blistering agents are liquids or gases that burn the skin. The mustard gas used in World War I is a blistering agent (Organization for the Prohibition of Chemical Weapons, 2000).

There are many advantages for terrorists who would like to use chemical or biological weapons. John Deutch (1996), former Director of the Central Intelligence Agency, believes the availability of chemical and biological weapons and the ease with which they can be transported make them the weapon of choice for terrorists who want to use WMDs. Jessica Stern (1998) says terrorists may use chemical and biological agents with crude delivery systems. In addition, Stern points out that the resulting panic caused by the use of such horrendous weapons will increase the aura of the group employing them.

While these weapons are horrific, many analysts feel they are inadequate substitutes for nuclear weapons. The reason is that there are more disadvantages than advantages. Leonard Cole (1996), one of the leading experts in the field of chemical and biological weapons, points out that these weapons are difficult to control.

Biological weapons virtually have no controls, and once they are introduced, the group using the weapon might well become a victim. For example, if a terrorist group was able to start a black plague epidemic in a major city, how could it stop the spread of the disease? In addition, it takes time for a biological agent to work. It must incubate, then spread from person to person. Most biological agents are destroyed by weather and sunlight. The agents that can survive, such as concentrated anthrax, are so lethal that they would threaten to contaminate their users for decades. According to Cole, biological weapons are unreliable.

Table 1: Chemical and Biological Agents

Types of Chemical Agents	Types of Biological Agents
Nerve	Natural poisons (ricin, saxitoxin, venom)
Blood	Viruses
Choking	Salmonella, botulism, anthrax
Blistering	Plagues

SOURCES: Canadian Intelligence Service and the Organization for the Prohibition of Chemical Weapons.

Chemical weapons are more readily controlled, but they are not as lethal. The FBI's Larry Mefford (1996) shows that chemical weapons are best used in a confined area. They would be an excellent choice for an attack on a building, but their effectiveness in mass destruction is limited. Despite these disadvantages, one should not assume that these weapons will not be used. Terrorists have access to chemical and biological weapons, they have used them, and will probably use them again.

Stephen Bowers and Kimberly Keys (1998) offer a sobering analysis of the likelihood of continued chemical and biological terrorism. Like many other analysts, Bowers and Keys believe the recent infusion of racism and religion in terrorist activities has changed the structure of modern terrorism. Religious zealots are more interested in destruction than the aura created by media coverage. Chemical and biological agents are attractive to such people.

Bowers and Keys propose a three-step methodology for approaching terrorism and technology. First, they argue that group profiling and behavioral analysis has been a powerful tool for counter-terrorism. To paraphrase a popular witticism among psychology professors, nothing predicts future behavior like past behavior. Bowers and Keys recommend that law enforcement and defense agencies aggressively analyze the behavior of terrorist groups in order to predict future behavior. Second, like Doug Bodrero, they recommend constant monitoring of social indicators. Terrorist groups do not develop overnight; they are produced by social forces. Law enforcement personnel must constantly monitor the social climate that produces violence. Finally, Bowers and Keys state a key point. Security personnel must share information. The days of FBI, CIA, and ATF rivalries are long gone. WMD threats make agency rivalries superfluous.

Law enforcement and the military can learn quite a bit about responding to WMDs from the firefighting service. Firefighters have dealt with chemical spills and biological disasters for decades. They have systems to identify and contain contaminated areas. Indeed, they already employ the biological and chemical detection systems used by the armed forces. Law enforcement, security, and military personnel can find a wealth of information on response at the National Fire Academy in Emmitsburg, Maryland.

Cyberterrorism

On January 22, 2000, President Clinton announced a billion dollar plan to fight cyberterrorism. The first question that came to many analysts of terrorism minds was: Is there a cyberterrorism? The answer is not clear. Former FBI counterterrorism specialist William Dyson (2000) perhaps gives the best answer. Dyson says computer terrorism is not a form of terrorism, but terrorists may use computers during the commission of terrorist acts.

Terrorists may use computers in a number of ways. Yael Shahar (1997) envisions scenarios where viruses are implanted in an enemy's computer. He also predicts "logic bombs" that lie dormant for years until they are instructed to overwhelm a computer system. Shahar also believes bogus chips can be sold to sabotage an enemy's computer network. Trojan horses can have a malevolent code to destroy a system, while back doors allow terrorists to enter "secure" systems. Shahar also believes conventional attacks such as overloading an electrical system serve to threaten computer security.

Michael Whine (1999) agrees with Shahar's conclusions, claiming that computer technology is attractive to terrorists for several reasons. Computers allow groups to remain connected, while allowing covert discussions and anonymity. Computer networks are also much less expensive and work intensive than the secretive infrastructures necessary to maintain terrorist groups. Computers also allow terrorists to reach their audiences with little effort. Whine concludes that computers are a force multiplier for terrorist groups.

Bowers and Keys (1998) believe cyberterrorism appears to be a threat because of the nature of modern society. Cyberterrorists may attack the infrastructure. In other words, they can destroy the underpinnings of the social base. Bowers and Keys believe this happens in terms of information flow. Since modern Western society functions on information, cyberterrorists threaten to interrupt or confuse the flow of information. Imagine, they say, an attack on the banking industry through the flow of fund information. Such an attack could completely devastate a society.

Bowers and Keys believe the ability of cyberterrorists to disrupt the economic system is matched by their ability to destroy confidence in social institutions. Cyberterrorists could make an audience feel as if their world is falling apart. Cyberterrorists can target health institutions as well as government services and businesses. They may even attack defense establishments.

By the same token, Bowers and Keys say cyberterrorism belongs to a broader category called "information warfare." Dyson (2000) agrees with all of these conclusions, and adds that terrorists even use the computer to train other terrorists. There is no doubt that computers are vulnerable to crime, and terrorists do use and will continue to use computers. In addition, Tiffany Danitz and Warren Strobel (1999) indicate that political activists can use the Internet as a command-and-control mechanism. Computer security is a necessity in commerce, government, and personal affairs. Terrorists, enemy military forces, criminals, hackers, and others will use computers to their advantage at the expense of others.

This excerpt has presented the most depressing aspect of modern terrorism, the megadeath and destruction that can be wrought by terrorists using technology. Yet, Dyson's point needs to be considered. Computers are tools used by terrorists. WMDs and other forms of technology represent the same thing. Perhaps there is no technological terrorism, but there are terrorists who will use technological weapons. Regardless of the terminology, it is a frightening scenario.

Part II: Religion and Terrorism

Religion is a system of beliefs, symbols, and rituals, based on some sacred or supernatural realm that guides human behavior, gives meaning to life, and unites believers into a community. Social Scientists study the role religion plays in society, how people become religious and the different forms of religious organizations. Religion has long played a crucial role in the development of social and political attitudes. In this part the following essays draw, again, from White, Terrorism: An Introduction, Fourth Edition, 2002 Update, *and from Joan Ferrante's text,* Sociology: The United States in a Global Community, Fourth Edition *(2000). Prof. Ferrante writes on religion with an emphasis on Afghanistan.*

A. Religion and Middle Eastern Terrorism
This excerpt was obtained from Jonathan R. White, *Terrorism: An Introduction*, Fourth Edition, 2002 Update (Wadsworth, 2003).

Middle Eastern terrorism is centered on the struggle for control of the area claimed by the Israelis and the Palestinians. Closely related to this issue is the spread of fundamentalist Islam beyond the Iranian Revolution. This struggle has appeared in three forms: struggle for control of the Palestinian movement, the directions of revolutionary Islam, and the spread of terrorism from the Afghan war. Since the mid-1990s, all three of these issues have been dominated by fervent religious fundamentalism. The Palestinian movement has been influenced by revolutionary Islam, especially from Hamas and Islamic Jihad. Other revolutionary groups are spreading in Egypt, Sudan, Pakistan, and Algeria. One of the main international threats comes from a group headed by Osama bin Ladin. Jewish fundamentalism has spawned its own anti-Arab terrorism. All of these violent extremist views threaten a very fragile peace process.

Two Views of Islam and Terrorism

The American view of Islam has been influenced by various presentations of Islamic extremism in the electronic media, and it has been influenced by popular misconceptions and stereotypes. Daniel Pipes (1983) wrote an outstanding theological and political analysis of Islam nearly 20 years ago. In an insightful summary of theological positions, Pipes demonstrates that many Western attitudes are incorrect. Islam is a legalistic religion more closely related to traditional Judaism than Pauline Christianity, even though all three religions worship the same God.

Unfortunately, Pipes's work did not receive the recognition and influence it deserved. If more policymakers had acted on Pipes's analysis, Americans may have found that many of their religious precepts match those found in Islam. Although most Muslims express religious concepts by combining theological and moral positions in political institutions, Islam is no more a religion of violent fanatics than Judaism or Christianity. Yet, many Americans have little knowledge of Islam. Today most Americans subscribe to one of two positions about Islam and terrorism.

Reuven Paz (1998) summarizes one particular position, but it can also be found in such journalistic examinations as Robin Wright (1986, 1989), Dilip Hiro (1987), and Amir Taheri (1987). This view states that Islamic fundamentalism is related to political violence in the Middle East. Paz pursues this further by asking the question: Is there an Islamic terrorism? His answer is yes.

Paz argues that Islam sees itself in a global war with the West. This is exacerbated by socioeconomic differences. Islamicists divide the world into the realm of Islam (dar al-Islam) and the realm of heresy (dar al-Harb). Islamic radicals have relegated the West to the realm of heresy. Paz says success against heresy is measured in the popular support of terrorist groups. Since Muslims in general see themselves in a struggle with the West for social and political reasons, Paz concludes that popular support of militant Islam indicates an "Islamic terrorism" exists. He says the West should not debate its existence, it should defend itself against Islamic terrorism.

Others are not so quick to accept such logic. David Kibble (1996) argues that Islamic fundamentalism seems to be a threat at face value. Radical groups of Islamics in Egypt, Saudi Arabia, Iran, and other areas appear to have declared war on the United States and its allies. Indeed, an American secretary of defense stated that Islamic fundamentalism is the greatest threat to American security since Communism. Kibble believes such fears are unfounded.

Kibble says there are pockets of Islamic extremism in the Middle East that sustain terrorism. He argues, however, that these segments are isolated and divided. There is a broad spectrum of religious and political beliefs in Islam that rejects violence. Kibble believes that when fundamentalists take power, it may be the first step toward democracy. He urges caution in labeling Middle Eastern violence as "Islamic terrorism."

Clarence Bouchat (1996) agrees. He says American fears and misunderstandings of Islam make it appear as if fundamentalists were united and threatening to gather the Middle East in a war against the West. This is not the case. Fundamentalists are a divided lot, just as religious fundamentalists in the United States are divided. The history of the West and the Middle East involves centuries of religious wars. Bouchat says more is to be gained by examining the religious similarities between the two regions than by using such terms as "Islamic terrorism."

It is quite clear that violent religious fanatics are playing key roles in Middle Eastern terrorism. This has resulted in a new type of terrorism in the region. In the 1990s, several international structures emerged in the name of religion. No longer relying on rogue states or the interests of competing nations, these groups have emerged as a cause unto themselves. Religion is the basis of their calling, and they attract followers throughout the region.

The Iranian Revolution and Hizbollah's Metamorphosis

When Israel invaded Lebanon in 1982, the Iranians responded by sending their Revolutionary Guards, creating and supporting a new terrorist network. At first glance, the connection seems to be an illogical geographical link, but closer examination reveals the purpose. The Israeli invasion prompted responses throughout the Muslim world, and the Iranians, hard-pressed to deal with their young revolutionaries at home, found a perfect place to export their unruly zeal. Locked in a large war with Iraq, the Iranians found Lebanon a place to fan the fires of revolution.

The name Hizbollah literally means "the Party of God." According to Dilip Hiro (1987, pp. 113–181, 240–243), Hizbollah grew out of the Iranian Revolution as an extension of the Revolutionary Guards. The Revolutionary Guards were the military wing of the Ayatollah Khomeini's organization. Hizbollah assisted the Revolutionary Guards by attempting to purify the revolution. It attacked all forms of Western thought and sought to consolidate Khomeini's gains.

Hiro says the members of Hizbollah were not only interested in carrying out the goals of the revolution, but also concerned with the social conditions of Islam in general. This helped account for their loose organizational structure. The Party of God was more a meeting of similar minds than a group interested in a rigid, formal structure. Shiaism was the heart of Hizbollah, and Shiites throughout the Middle East were the concern of the group. The Shiites of Lebanon were no exception. Wege (1994) adequately demonstrates Hiro's argument. The term Party of God is taken from Islamic references and is directly related to the martyrdom of Hussein Ibn Ali. Failure to understand Hizbollah as an Islamic concept is a failure to understand the context of evangelical Islam.

According to Hiro, relations between Lebanese and Iranian Shiites had been close since the 1950s. When conflict broke out in Lebanon in 1975, Amal—a Shiite militia—was formed to protect Lebanese Shiites. Amal was trained by the PLO, but it developed and maintained strong Iranian contacts. In 1979, it grew in strength, and its members watched the Iranian Revolution with interest.

According to Anat Kurz (1994), Palestinian and Lebanese radicals found common ground in the 1980s. Nabih Berri was elected general secretary of Amal in 1980. This event caused concern among the more radical members of Amal, including those who supported the Iranian Revolution, because they believed Berri was a constitutionalist and too conservative. In 1982, the radicals left Amal for the Syrian-controlled Bekaa Valley, where they formed a new group, Islamic Amal, and awaited further developments. When the first Revolutionary Guards of Hizbollah arrived in the Bekaa Valley in 1982, they found willing allies in the Islamic Amal.

For the first few years of its involvement, Hizbollah acted more or less like a terrorist clearinghouse (Reuters, 1996a). Following orders from Iran, Hizbollah met as an independent organization, always willing to deny its Iranian connections. According to Israeli intelligence (Israeli Foreign Ministry, 1996), Hizbollah was directed by three central figures: Sheik Mohammed Hussein Fadlollah, Abus Musawi, and Hassan Nasrallah. Fadlollah, the target of an attempted American-sponsored assassination, was a charismatic spiritual leader. Nasrallah was a practical militarist, leaving the Islamic Amal militia to organize Hizbollah into a regional force. Musawi provided the loose connections to Iran.

From 1982 to 1985, Hizbollah formed a relationship with a shadowy terrorist group known as Islamic Jihad. According to Amir Tehari (1987), Hizbollah leaders met to give policy direction for Islamic Jihad. The council of leaders met in the city of Baalbek in Lebanon's Bekaa Valley and issued nebulous "suggestions" to Islamic Jihad. They also provided financial and logistical support for terrorist operations but kept themselves out of the day-to-day affairs of the terrorist group. By keeping their distance, Hizbollah's leaders were able to claim they had no direct knowledge of Islamic Jihad, and more importantly, they kept Iran from being directly linked to Islamic Jihad's terrorist campaign against Israel and the West.

During this same time frame, Hizbollah's role also began to change. As part of an organization designed to spread the Shiite revolution, Hizbollah was not content to act only as an umbrella group to support terrorism (Enteshami, 1995; Reuters, 1996a). Its leaders wanted to develop a revolutionary movement similar to the structure that gripped Iran in 1978 and 1979. Lebanon was inundated with several militias fighting for control of the government, and Nasrallah saw an opportunity. By following the pattern of the Amal militia, he began changing the structure of Hizbollah. In 1985, he established regional centers, transforming them to operational bases between 1987 and 1989. Taking over the organization after the death of Musawi, Nasrallah created a regional militia by 1990. In 1991, many of Lebanon's roving paramilitary groups signed a peace treaty, but Hizbollah retained its weapons and revolutionary philosophy. It became the primary paramilitary force in southern Lebanon (U.S. Department of State, 1996).

According to an analysis by Reuters (1996b), Hizbollah is currently fighting an undeclared war with Israel (see Table 2 for a sampling of its paramilitary activities). Vowing to disrupt the peace process and continue the revolution, members strike Israel in a style reminiscent of the early days of Fatah. The terrorist group it once commanded, the Islamic Jihad, has expanded and taken on a life of its own. Although Hizbollah conducts its own terrorist operations, it behaves more like a militia seeking control of Lebanon. Because most of the Lebanese militias were disarmed in 1991, Hizbollah's triumph in keeping its structure and weapons, have placed it in a position of power. LikeAbu Nidal, its structure allows it to act as a power broker in a world of shadow warfare.

By the same token, the paramilitary structure of Hizbollah has made it more of a conventional fighting force than a terrorist group since 1991. This results in a particular type of fighting. Unlike Islamic Jihad or the Abu Nidal group, Hizbollah's bases are in the open. When it strikes Israel, the Israeli Defense Force strikes back. Civilians caught in the crossfire are often at the mercy of opposing factions. In one tragic exchange, Israeli artillery shells hit a Palestinian village in April 1996, even though the shells were aimed at Hizbollah rocket launchers. Unfortunately, this type of exchange is nothing new to the area.

TABLE 2	A Sampling of Hizbollah's Paramilitary Activities
December 1995 -	Hizbollah fires rockets from Lebanon into Israel.
February 1996 -	Terrorists try to infiltrate Israel in ultralight aircraft.
March 1996 -	Hizbollah plants several bombs around Israeli targets; militias ambush Israeli convoys and settlement; more rocket attacks on Israel.
April 1996 -	Rocket attacks on civilians in Galilee; Israel returns fire and hits innocent Palestinians.

SOURCE: Israeli Foreign Ministry, April 1996.

The Islamic Jihad

Although Hizbollah found an ally in the Islamic Jihad when it came to the Bekaa Valley in 1982, the Iranian Revolution was not directly responsible for the birth of this terrorist group. Islamic Jihad began as a political movement inside the Muslim Brotherhood. Actually, there are several Islamic Jihads, and they are mostly nationalistic factions of the same movement. The group that receives greatest attention emerged after the 1982 Israeli invasion of Lebanon, and it came from the link with Hizbollah. This Islamic Jihad perfected three tactical innovations of terrorism: a dynamic "umbrella" organizational structure, the use of suicide bombers, and the shift away from hijackings and hostage-takings to individual kidnappings.

According to official Israeli reports (Israeli Foreign Ministry, 1996), Lebanon's Islamic Jihad was born in Israel and is currently commanded from Syria. Its leader, Dr. Fathi Shekaki, created the group in 1981. After the Israeli invasion of Lebanon, his fanatics flocked to Hizbollah and Hassan Fadlollah, the spiritual leader of Hizbollah. Shekaki and Fadlollah were immediately attracted to one another by similar visions, and Fadlollah brought Shekaki's organization under Hizbollah's umbrella.

The Israeli Foreign Ministry states that Shekaki participated in the "conference management" style of Hizbollah but took the organizational structure a step further. If Musawi and Nasrallah (the two leaders of Hizbollah) were looking for distance between terrorist activities and Iran, Shekaki saw the Hizbollah model as a new method for structuring terrorism. Rather than operating as a single entity, he broke Islamic Jihad into a multitude of smaller groups, creating distance between any terrorist act and the terrorist group. Each operation could literally have its own small terrorist group, and Islamic Jihad could hide in a flow of misinformation. In actuality, Shekaki's Islamic Jihad became an umbrella group, itself under the umbrella of Hizbollah.

Robin Wright (1986, pp. 84–86) writes that the structure of Islamic Jihad was different than anything the West had ever faced before. Most groups could be identified by an infrastructure and a support network. This was not the case with Islamic Jihad. It was a dynamic network distributing information from the secrecy of Baalbek. It contained a fluctuating number of secret organizations and cells. Although U.S. officials talked of state-sponsored terrorism, this group had no clear links to Iran. Islamic Jihad was a hidden army. As a result, its structure confused Western intelligence sources for nearly a decade.

To strike, Shekaki chose a new weapon: the suicide bomber. Amir Taheri (1987) states that after the first suicide bombing in 1983, Islamic Jihad launched a devastating suicide bombing campaign in Lebanon. In 1984, its activities spread to Kuwait and Tunisia, and it became clear that the struggle was not just for Lebanon but also for the Islamic revolution. By 1986, in Taheri's estimation, fighting had moved to Europe. This brand of international terrorism is endorsed because it involves a holy war against all parties resisting the Islamic revolution. Taheri refers to it as the "holy terror."

The use of suicide bombers frightened and baffled the West, but it was logically explicable in terms of the conflict, according to Maxwell Taylor and Helen Ryan (1988). Taylor and Ryan examine the role of fanaticism in Shiite terrorism and conclude that the use of suicide bombers was particularly successful in Lebanon. A suicide bomber became an inexpensive guided missile ensuring the success of an attack.

After a series of bombings in 1983 and the retreat of the U.S. Marines from Beirut, the weakness of Western defensive systems was completely exposed. Military forces from France, Israel, and the United States had employed a fairly sophisticated security system appropriate to peacekeeping situations in Western diplomacy. In several instances, suicide bombers penetrated these defensive perimeters and struck targets with relative ease. Taylor and Ryan suggest this demonstrates a fundamental weakness of technologically based defense: None of the defenders had predicted the role of suicide in the Lebanese conflict.

Taylor and Ryan argue it is necessary to define terrorism in Middle Eastern terms rather than to extrapolate from Western norms. From the Western perspective, suicide attacks seem rooted in illogical fanaticism. Yet, this interpretation does not fit the Shiites fighting in Lebanon. Bombing was a logical policy—in fact, one of the few policies that worked against established military power. Because delivery of the bombs had to be guaranteed if the policy was to work, it was also logical to employ sacrificial warriors as delivery sources.

Shekaki also used another tactic, kidnapping. The development of specialized hostage rescue teams in the United States, Great Britain, and Germany forced Islamic Jihad to search for new hostage-taking tactics. Airplanes were hijacked, but hostages had to be dispersed. New Western rescue units, such as the British Special Air Service, the German GSG-9, and the American Delta Force, made traditional methods of taking hostages too risky. Kidnapping developed as an attractive alternative to massive hostage taking. Counterterrorist forces might be able to free hostages in a single incident, but dispersed kidnapping victims were another issue.

Islamic Jihad toyed with the idea of kidnapping in 1983, and by the next year, they launched a wholesale kidnapping campaign. At one point, they held more than 40 Western hostages. Hizbollah and Islamic Jihad saw they could not only gain the attention of the West with kidnappings, but also influence the behavior of Western governments.

The kidnapping policy of Islamic Jihad had several practical functions. It could be used to punish a country for acting against the Shiites. Hostages could be released for propaganda value, or, when an enemy took action against Islamic Jihad or its supporters, hostages could be executed. Finally, threats of harm to hostages or additional kidnappings could be used to influence another government's actions.

Tactical innovation came as a surprise to the West. In a special article prepared for the New York Times, Philip Taubman (1984) writes that the United States had few solid leads on the Islamic Jihad, despite enhanced intelligence efforts. In a related article, Eric Pace (1984) describes the innovative use of car bombs in the Middle East. The West seemed at a tactical loss when dealing with Islamic Jihad. The Israelis took a different approach. Instead of mapping the hierarchy and flow of money, Israel identified the group's leaders and went after them.

The Israeli Foreign Ministry (1996) says Shekaki was captured and deported in 1988, but he resurfaced in Damascus in 1989. In the aftermath of the Persian Gulf War, Islamic Jihad moved its activities to Israel. Directing operations from Syria, Shekaki continued the struggle against Israel. When Arafat accepted the Israeli olive branch and elections in the occupied territories, Shekaki abandoned support for the Intifada (a general uprising) and returned to terrorism.

Shekaki addressed the issue in an interview with Time magazine (1995). He spoke of no peace until Israel was destroyed. He also reiterated his willingness to employ human-guided missiles, the suicide bombers. Unlike Hamas, he stated that Islamic Jihad was willing to accept a liberated Palestine devoid of a united Arab realm. The U.S. Department of State (1996) took such statements at face value, pointing to threats for an expanded suicide bombing campaign in 1995. Shekaki was killed in Malta in 1995.

Shekaki's successor, Dr. Ramadan Abdallah Sallah, has maintained the Shekaki philosophy. The Israeli Foreign Ministry (1996) says that as of 1992, Islamic Jihad is no longer able to hide as easily as it could in its early stages. Israeli and Western intelligence agencies have developed internal profiles of the group, and some of its leaders are known. More importantly, the growth and emergence of Hizbollah removed the umbrella covering of Islamic Jihad. The Shekaki faction was forced to operate like most other terrorist groups.

Following elections in the occupied territories, Islamic Jihad, like Hamas and Hizbollah, began a no-holds-barred campaign to disrupt the peace process. Israeli soldiers were kidnapped and executed, and bombings increased. The Israelis responded with controversial measures. Specialized squadrons of selected soldiers would raid suspected terrorist hideouts. Under this policy, suspects were interned while all their resources, including their homes, and the resources of their supporters were destroyed. Several suspected terrorists had been killed during these operations, and hundreds of homes were bulldozed into the ground.

The U.S. Department of State (1996) sums up Islamic Jihad's threat well. The State Department says it is a loose affiliation of several fanatical groups. It still probably receives aid from Iran, but the convoluted nature of the group makes it difficult to expose. Islamic Jihad does not have a hierarchy or infrastructure similar to other groups. Because it is so loosely bound, any one of the many groups may act autonomously.

Hamas

One of the most volatile militant organizations in the Middle East is the Islamic Resistance Movement, better known as Hamas. Unlike Hizbollah and Islamic Jihad, it grew from the Palestinian movement. Mirroring the philosophy of the Rejectionists, Hamas' position is that the state of Israel should not exist. The only acceptable solution to the Palestinian problem is to eliminate Israel and create a united Arab realm. According to Hamas, the state of Israel and anyone who supports it are abominations to Islam.

To understand Hamas, it is necessary to go back to the events right after World War I. Because of the British promises, many Arabs felt that the entire Middle East, from North Africa to the Iranian border, would be united under one great Arabic banner, dar al-Islam. When European powers divided the area, taking control of some regions and placing their Arab allies in control of others, many Arabs were infuriated. One group of frustrated Muslims took action. Founded in Egypt about 1925, the Muslim Brotherhood rejected the new territorial lines. They called for unification of the entire Arab realm under the law and control of Islam.

In 1967, the Muslim Brotherhood began to grow in the occupied territories. Unlike the Ba'athists who expressed unity through modern socialism, followers of the Muslim Brotherhood wanted to purify Islam and unite with other Arabs under religious law. In some ways, the philosophy of the Muslim Brotherhood was a combination of the religious intensity of the Iranian Revolution and the unification principles of the Ba'athists, but the Muslim Brotherhood primarily represented ethnicity more than politics or religion. Their call for unity was as old as the Q'ran.

The group registered as a religious organization with the Israeli government in 1978, and its stated purpose was to be evangelical. Members attempted to convert followers into a more pristine version of Islam. They worked through universities, schools, and mosques. In the 1980s, however, as Arafat gravitated toward moderation, the Muslim Brotherhood maintained its rigid views on the unification of the realm of Arabs and the necessity to rule through Islamic law. When the demand for Palestinian self-government began to dominate the Palestinian movement, the Muslim Brotherhood rejected the call.

Self-government was abhorrent to the Muslim Brotherhood because no nation should exist outside dar al-Islam. If the fedayeen of Fatah were to betray their people by talk of compromise, the Muslim Brotherhood would take a different path. As a result of their disagreement with the goals of the Intifada, members of the Muslim Brotherhood formed Hamas, an Arabic acronym for the Islamic Resistance Movement, in 1987.The group has been active ever since.

Following the tactics of the old Irgun, Hamas has attempted to outdo former Palestinian terrorists. In its own literature, Hamas says that it is in a war with the Jewish people, as well as the state of Israel. The purpose of every operation is to kill Jews, and by killing Jews, all the Zionist settlers and their allies will be driven from the area. It is not enough to kill only the Jews, however. "Good" Muslims will kill anyone who accepts peace with the Jews or who speaks of an independent Palestine. The only acceptable outcome for Hamas is the united realm of Islam.

Hamas is well financed and organized. As any large terrorist organization, it is composed of strike units, as well as logistical support columns. Its tentacles reach far outside the Middle East, including support bases in the United States. Ironically, its size has caused a moderate group to emerge from the ranks of the fanatics. Arafat has tried desperately to work with the moderates to stop the spread of terrorism. The goal of Hamas terrorists is to disrupt the peace process. They may succeed. Since 1989, they have been responsible for several hundred terrorist attacks.

Being a large organization, tens of thousands strong according to a 1996 State Department estimate, Hamas has a centralized structure with many branches. According to Ahmad Rashad (1996), an apologist for the group, Hamas's strength comes from Palestinian dissatisfaction with the PLO. Rashad states Arafat's softened attitude toward Israel prompted the rise of Hamas in 1987. As enthusiasm grew, Hamas's goal was to become the sole representative of the Palestinian people. Accordingly, it divided its operations into four main spheres: administration, charity, politics, and military affairs.

Rashad states that the most successful military actions have been taken by the Izz el-Din al-Qassam Brigades. Emerging from the military wing of Hamas, the al-Qassam Brigades swelled with recruits after Arafat's renunciation of terrorism in 1993. The brigades are divided into two factions: an intelligence wing and a commando wing.

Ironically, according to Rashad, the intelligence wing does not gather military intelligence. If Rashad is to be believed, the intelligence wing serves as an internal police force. It has three primary duties. First, it enforces Islamic law among the Palestinians, including the execution of offenders. Second, it serves as the main instrument for distributing propaganda throughout the occupied territories. Finally and very interestingly, it is the logistical support network for military operations. Reading through Rashad's propaganda, it is safe to assume the intelligence wing is designed for internal discipline and to supply and hide active terrorists.

The commando wing is designed for terrorist attacks, and it has three primary sections: training, operations, and intelligence. Rashad did not mention bombing or ambushes, two al-Qassam Brigade specialties, but he pointed with pride to "the abduction of enemy soldiers." This admission is quite appropriate. Taking a page from lessons in Lebanon, Hamas has kidnapped and executed individual Israeli soldiers. Although he refuses to identify the total number of commando units, Rashad identifies two groups that operated in the occupied territories and states the remaining groups functioned at large. In essence, the military wing is organized in the manner of any large terrorist group.

Hamas represents the continuing struggle for control of the Palestinian voice. Whereas the PLO has rejected terrorism, Hamas has embraced it, and it has become a rallying point for those wishing to continue the struggle with Israel. If anything, Hamas represents the issue so aptly identified by Ahmad Khalidi (1995). There can be no end to terrorism, Khalidi says, until the rights of Palestinians are guaranteed. Hamas will certainly maintain its appeal to disenfranchised Palestinians until that time.

The Rise of Osama Bin Ladin

To understand the rise of Osama bin Ladin, it is necessary to keep two things in mind. First, there is a trend among Islamic fundamentalists to attempt to bridge the theological gap between Sunnis and Shiites. This trend began to develop in Iran about 1988. According to Dov Waxman (1998), Iran has moved from a postrevolutionary, nationalist phase to the real politics of pan- Islam. That is, Iranian leaders slowly moved away from their blind allegiance to Shiaism and began supporting militant Sunnis. Revolutionary Iranians began sending money and support to Sunni terrorist groups in Lebanon, believing Iranian Shiites and Lebanese Sunnis were working for the same cause. Militant Sunnis followed suit, calling for peace between Sunnis and Shiites. Osama bin Ladin, a Saudi Arabian, was one such Sunni.

The second important factor in the rise of bin Ladin was the Soviet- Afghan War (1979–1989). In 1979, the Soviet Union invaded Afghanistan. Seven major guerrilla groups formed to resist the Soviets, and the United States enthusiastically joined the fray with arms and economic support. The resistance fighters called themselves the Holy Warriors, the mujahadeen. Embraced by the U.S. government, they traveled the United States calling the Soviets "foreign devils" and "infidels." Few of Ronald Reagan's political leaders noticed that the mujahadeen leaders used the same terms to describe Americans.

In 1989, the Soviets retreated from Afghanistan in complete disarray. Not only had they lost the war, but the Soviet Union also soon found itself in a state of collapse. Yael Shahar (1998) says the mujahadeen saw the fall of the Soviet Union as a sign of total victory. The Soviet Union had not collapsed under the weight of political, economic, and military factors, but in the minds of the mujahadeen, it fell by the hand of God. The Soviet retreat was a sign of God's power over Satan, and if God could bring down the Soviet Union through the work of the mujahadeen, other evil nations were doomed to destruction. The primary targets of the mujahadeen were Israel and the United States. One of the mujahadeen leaders who fervently believes in this view is Osama bin Ladin.

Yosseff Bodansky (1999) writes the most detailed biography of bin Ladin, although the work is polemical and does not seek objectivity. Bodansky says bin Ladin was one of 51 children born to a rich Saudi Arabian construction magnate in 1957. Bin Ladin received a university education and joined the family business, but he soon left Saudi Arabia to join the Afghan fight against the Soviet Union. At first, he lent support to the mujahadeen, later forming his own unit of guerrilla fighters.

While in Afghanistan, he fell under the influence of Sheik Abdullah Azzam, a doctor of Sharia (Islamic law). Azzam had been working for the Palestinians in the mid-1970s, but he became disillusioned with their nationalism and emphasis of politics over religion. Azzam believed Islam should rule over all forms of conflict. He left the Palestinians for a Saudi university to teach Islamic law.

Azzam was the answer to bin Ladin's prayers. As the rich Saudi construction engineer sought a path to holy war, he found the theology of Azzam to his liking. According to Azzam, the realm of Islam had been dominated by foreign powers for too long. It was time for all Muslims to rise up and strike Satan. The Soviet-Afghan War was just the beginning. The mujahadeen were in a holy war against all things foreign to Islam.

Bodansky points out the United States would hardly have been excited about funding such a group of rebels, but the Pakistani Intelligence Service (ISI) intervened. The ISI was concerned with the growing threat of the Soviet Union, but it had its own agenda for national security. Pakistan offered to act as the surrogate for the United States, training the mujahadeen and providing their base camps. According to Bodansky, all money, weapons, and other logistics would be funneled through the ISI. The American Central Intelligence Agency took the bait, and the ISI prepared for war against America's enemy. It also prepared for a larger war without telling the CIA.

Osama bin Ladin was in the midst of these activities. Training in Pakistan and Afghanistan, he financed mujahadeen operations and taught the guerrillas how to build field fortifications. By 1986, he left the training field for the battlefield. Enraged with the Soviets for their wholesale slaughter of Afghan villagers and use of poison gas, bin Ladin joined the front ranks of the mujahadeen. Allied with hundreds of radical militants throughout the world, Osama bin Ladin became a battlefield hero. When interviewed for ABC News by John Miller (1998), bin Ladin would not discuss these exploits. He simply stated that all Muslims are required to fight in the jihad.

The ISI was spreading the jihad. Bodansky argues that while watching the disputed Kashmir province (an area claimed by both India and Pakistan), leaders from the ISI were not content to limit their war to the Soviet Union. In 1986, the ISI began filtering some of the arms intended for the mujahadeen to Sikh terrorists in India. When this diversion was successful, the ISI began filtering arms and logistics to Muslim militants in Kashmir. Bodanksy says Shiite militants in Iran noticed the ISI actions and began to view the Afghan war as an expression of Islamic unity. In the meantime, Pakistan began to see itself as a leader in the pan-Arabic movement.

Things did not go as well for Azzam. When the Soviets were preparing to withdraw, the ISI created its own Afghan guerrilla force and used it to take control of major areas of Afghanistan. Azzam believed the United States was behind this action. Before he could take action on his own, he was killed in a terrorist attack by unknown assailants. Bin Ladin accepted the status quo and enjoyed warm relations with the ISI. He returned to Saudi Arabia after the war to resume his construction business.

The Saudi Arabian government was not too happy to see bin Ladin return. Not attractive to the Saudi royal family, bin Ladin was immensely popular with the people. Saudi Arabia is not an open democracy that tolerates diverse opinions and dissension; thus, bin Ladin's political activities were limited. He brought several mujahadeen-his "Afghans"-to Saudi Arabia with him and put them to work on construction projects. The Afghans had job security, and bin Ladin became independently wealthy.

The situation changed in 1990. Saudi Arabia houses two of the most holy shrines in Islam, the cities of Mecca and Medina. To millions of Muslims, including bin Ladin, these are sacred areas that must be protected by Muslims. This is considered holy ground. In 1990, Saddam Hussein, leader of Iraq, invaded Kuwait. The Saudi royal family appealed for help, and thousands of non-Muslim troops arrived in the holy land to fight Saddam Hussein. The American-led coalition called this military buildup "Desert Shield." When "Desert Shield" became "Desert Storm" in February 1991, radical Muslims were appalled to find Muslims fighting Muslims under American leadership. After the war, the Saudi government allowed American troops to be stationed in Saudi Arabia. This was too much for bin Ladin. He thought of declaring his own war.

Bodansky says bin Ladin was influenced by the pan-Islamic movement and the role of Iran. Putting aside differences between Shiites and Sunnis, radical Muslims found Satan arrayed against Islam; Satan came in the form of the United States. Bin Ladin worked with the Iranians to bring eschatological Sunnis and Shiites together in an organization called the International Muslim Brotherhood, but he wanted to go further. By April, he was training and financing terrorist groups and calling for the overthrow of unsympathetic Muslim governments.

PBS *Front Line* (1998) says these actions brought a Saudi crackdown, and bin Ladin was forced to flee. He first went to Afghanistan and then to Sudan. Bodansky states bin Ladin found friends in the radical government of Sudan, and he expanded his operations. By the end of 1992, bin Ladin had nearly 500 Afghans working for businesses that he established in Sudan. He also saw internationalism as the best means for striking the United States, and he refused to base his operations in any single country. In December 1992, a bomb exploded in a hotel in Yemen, a hotel that had been housing American troops. *Front Line* says U.S. intelligence linked the attack to bin Ladin.

Declaring War on the United States

Osama bin Ladin redefined the meaning of terrorism in the modern world. To understand this, it is helpful to compare his movement to the Palestinian movement. The PLO tried to become a state military organization, and it failed. It first operated in Jordan, then Lebanon, then Tunisia, and finally it renounced terrorism. Violence could only be carried out by splinter criminal groups on a subnational level, and these groups could not be controlled by the PLO. Abu Nidal's version of terrorism, on the other hand, used multiple support bases for Palestinian radicals. Instead of becoming a state, he moved within many states with many different types of organizations, eventually hiring out his terrorists to state supporters. Osama bin Ladin differs in his approach from both forms of violence. With the wealth of his construction empire as backing, bin Ladin transcended the state and operated on his own.

Yael Shahar (1998) argues bin Ladin's entrepreneurial efforts give him the freedom to finance and command his own terror network. His connections with his Afghans and his reputation as a warrior give him legitimacy. Bin Ladin does not need a government to support his operations. He has the money, personnel, material, and infrastructure necessary to maintain a campaign of terrorism. He only needs a place to hide.

According to *Front Line*, bin Ladin went on the offensive in 1993. Using his contacts in Sudan, he began searching for weapons of mass destruction. His Afghans sought to purchase nuclear weapons from underground sources in the Russian Federation, and he began work on a chemical munitions plant in Sudan. Bodansky says he also sent terrorists to fight in other parts of the world. Bin Ladin's Afghans went to Algeria, Egypt, Bosnia, Pakistan, Somalia, Kashmir, and Chechnya. U.S. intelligence sources also believe they came to the United States, and they linked him to the 1993 World Trade Center bombing.

Bin Ladin was active in Somalia when American troops joined an endemic civil war to bring food to the area. In October 1993, a U.S. Army Black Hawk helicopter was downed while on patrol in Mogadishu. U.S. Army Rangers went to the rescue, and a two-day battle ensued in which 18 Americans lost their lives. In an interview with *ABC News*'s John Miller, bin Ladin claimed he trained and supported the troops that struck the Americans.

Bin Ladin was also involved in assassination attempts. In 1993, his Afghans tried to murder Prince Abdullah of Jordan. In 1995, U.S. intelligence sources believe he was behind the attempted assassination of Egyptian President Hosni Mubarak. According to *Front Line*, bin Ladin called for a guerrilla campaign against Americans in Saudi Arabia in 1995.

Bombing also entered bin Ladin's arsenal of mayhem. In 1995, his Afghans killed five American service personnel and two Indian soldiers with a truck bombing in Riyadh, Saudi Arabia. In 1996, he struck in Dharan, killing 19 Americans with another truck bomb. Bin Ladin called his group of Afghans, al-Qaeda or The Base.

Bin Ladin followed these actions by calling for a holy war against the United States and its allies. In 1996, Osama bin Ladin officially "declared war" on the United States. He followed this by two religious rulings, called fatwas, in 1998. Magnus Ranstorp (1998) argues these writings reveal quite a bit about the nature of al-Qaeda and bin Ladin. First, bin Ladin represents a new phase in Middle Eastern terrorism. He is intent on spreading the realm of Islam with a transnational group. Second, he uses Islam to call for religious violence. Bin Ladin is a self-trained religious fanatic ready to kill in the name of God. Finally, bin Ladin wants to bring death. Whether with conventional weapons or weapons of mass destruction, bin Ladin's purpose is to kill. In his fatwa of February 1998, he calls for the killing of any American anywhere in the world.

In August 1998, bin Ladin's terrorists were behind two horrendous attacks in Africa, bombing the American embassies in Nairobi, Kenya, and Dar es Salaam, Tanzania. The Nairobi bomb killed 213 people and injured 4,500. The Dar es Salaam explosion killed 12 and wounded 85. An FBI investigative report gives an indication of bin Ladin's methods.

Bin Ladin's Bombings

Bombing has been one of Osama bin Ladin's primary terrorist tactics. He has been linked to the 1993 New York City World Trade Center bombing, a bombing in Kuwait, and three bombings targeting American military personnel. Despite his involvement in murder, no one was prepared for the attacks he launched on August 7, 1998. Bin Ladin's attacks in Nairobi and Dar es Salaam drew the attention of the world.

According to the FBI (2000), Osama bin Ladin and Mohammed Atef began planning an East African operation against the United States after American intervention in Somalia in 1992 and 1993. Atef, who runs the military and training wing of al-Qaeda, began building an infrastructure for a terrorist bombing in Kenya about 1994, with the assistance of Wadih El-Hage, an American citizen from Texas. Another group under the leadership of Abu Ubaida, one of bin Ladin's associates, established a base in Tanzania. Both groups purchased houses with a large garage and a high fence surrounding the property. Both of these bases served to hide the activities of the terrorists.

In Nairobi, the terrorists assembled a team, including a military leader, bomb technicians, truck drivers, and weapons specialists. The initial plan was to attack the embassy with a truck and two terrorists. One terrorist was to frighten Kenyans away from the perimeter of the embassy building, while the other was to drive the bomb-laden truck inside. The primary explosive agent was TNT. When the truck approached, the driver and his assistant found the driveway blocked. The assistant fled the scene, while the driver committed suicide by detonating the bomb. The terrorist succeeded in creating much property damage, but the human carnage was horrific. Although bin Ladin's terrorists wanted to murder Americans, they managed to kill or maim most of the Kenyans who happened to be passing by the embassy, only killing a few Americans.

A similar team was assembled in Tanzania, except the plan called for a single suicide bomber. Once again, the team used a house surrounded by a privacy fence to plan the attack. The terrorists made no attempt to warn Tanzanians in the area. Shortly after the attack in Nairobi, a single terrorist drove a truck loaded with explosives to the U.S. embassy in Dar es Salaam and detonated the bomb. This time bin Ladin's group only murdered Tanzanians. No Americans were killed.

The ambiguity of American counterterrorist policy emerged in the wake of the bombing. Was this a military matter, or should it be handled as a breach of international law? The United States responded in two ways. First, FBI antiterrorist task forces composed of federal agents, state, and local police officers went to both scenes. In the subsequent investigation, two arrests were made and a fuller picture of al-Qaeda began to emerge. Task force investigators testified before a federal grand jury and arrest warrants were issued for bin Ladin, Atef, and other members of al-Qaeda.

President Clinton, however, had another response as well. Armed with intelligence of possible locations of bin Ladin's bases, and with possible evidence of chemical weapons production in Sudan, Clinton ordered a cruise missile attack against selected targets. The missiles destroyed a factory in Sudan, although subsequent reports questioned the material being produced there, and missiles also landed on six bases in Afghanistan. Bin Ladin escaped. Critics claimed these actions were designed to divert attention from Clinton's impending impeachment trial. Regardless, the cruise missiles symbolized a substantial departure from the antiterrorism task force's legalistic approach to the bombings.

Bin Ladin remains popular among Muslim radicals. He has established links with Egyptian terrorist groups and has sent his Afghans to many different countries. In June 2000, his followers began launching suicide bombings against Russian soldiers in Chechnya. Ranstorp (1998) argues bin Ladin will eventually tumble because his theological tirades do not reflect the basis of Islam. He is theologically untrained and does not enjoy the support of Muslim clerics. Today, bin Ladin remains the most wanted man in the world. If he is allowed to operate in a new territory, there is very little question he will continue terrorist operations, and American planners need to ask the question: Do we handle bin Ladin as a military or law enforcement problem?

B. A Sociological Look at the Role of Religion in Afghanistan

The excerpt was written by Joan Ferrante, Sociology: A Global Perspective, Fifth Edition (Wadsworth, 2003).

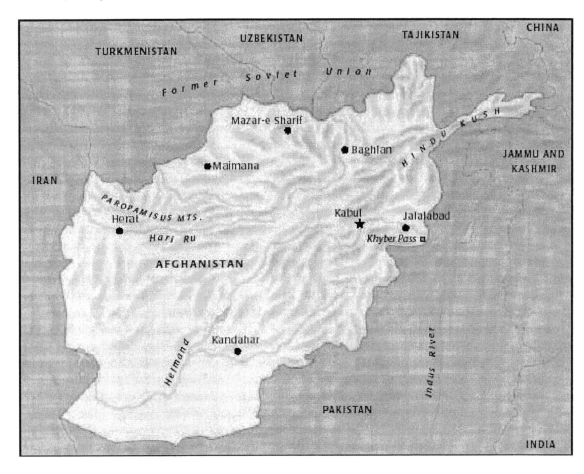

The Historical Context

Before the nineteenth century, mountainous Afghanistan lay in the path of invaders from China, Persia (ancient Iran), and the Indian subcontinent. In the nineteenth and twentieth centuries, the country became a battleground for the British and Russian empires and, after World War II, for the United States and the Soviet Union. In 1979, the Soviet Union invaded Afghanistan to support a secular government.

Supported materially by the United States, Afghanistan's military resistance to the Soviets was mobilized in large part through religious institutions that proclaimed a "holy war." The Soviet exit in 1989 left a ravaged country full of religiously charged armed rival factions. When the Taliban government took power in 1996, it justified many of its new policies on religious Islamic grounds. Westerners tend to see such policies as simply fanatical and irrational and to overlook the histories that led up to them. They also tend to disregard the parallels that can be drawn between the role of religion in Afghan society and its significant role in our own.

In explaining how sociologists view and study religion as an aspect of social life, this section helps us make sense of events in Afghanistan.

Why Focus on Afghanistan?

At the time of this writing, the Northern Alliance, supported by U.S. military airpower, had overthrown the Taliban, an Islamic fundamentalist group that took control of the country in 1996. After coming to power, the Taliban received headline news coverage focusing on the strict and harsh version of Islamic law it imposed on the local populations. Since September 11, 2001, media coverage emphasized the Taliban's connection to Osama bin Laden and to what is known in the West as the al-Qaida network. For the most part, the news has focused on the immediate situation, neglecting the larger historical context that gave rise to the Taliban and to al-Qaida.

The images of real repression and violence are consistent with the "snapshot" images that many Americans associate with the Muslim religion, or Islam. For many, the term "Islam" evokes images of the November 1995 explosion of a U.S. military training and communication center in Riyadh, the capital of Saudi Arabia; the 1993 World Trade Center bombings in New York City; the 1988 bombing of Pan Am Flight 103 over Lockerbee, Scotland; the stepped-up airport security in the wake of the Gulf War with Iraq in 1991; and the commercial aircraft-turned-cruise-missile bombings of the World Trade Center towers and the Pentagon.

Whatever the event, one idea seems to dominate the coverage: some Islamic group—the Movement of Islamic Amal, the Islamic Jehad organization, the Hezbollah (Party of God), the al-Qaida—is responsible. In other words, each event becomes reduced to the actions of religious fanatics acting solely from "primitive and irrational" religious conviction. This perspective masks more important political, geographic, and economic factors and causes viewers to lose sight of the larger questions: Is the Taliban's version of Islamic law consistent with "Islamic principles?" How did the Taliban rise to power in Afghanistan? How did the al-Qaida network come to be connected with Afghanistan? Why does the religious affiliation of the Taliban and of al-Qaida members receive more attention than the social, economic, and political factors driving their policies and actions?

In this excerpt, we consider the answers to these questions and more. In doing so, we will come to realize that religious affiliation explains little about the causes behind terrorist acts or wars against terrorism. Rather, the social, economic, and political circumstances that cause people to draw upon religion to justify responses defined as terrorism are far more revealing than knowledge of a group's religious affiliation. We will examine religion from a sociological perspective. Such a perspective is useful because it allows us to step back and view, in a detached way, an often emotion-charged subject. Detachment and objectivity are necessary if we wish to avoid making sweeping generalizations about the nature of religions, such as Islam, that are unfamiliar to many of us.

When sociologists study religion, they do not investigate whether God or some other supernatural force exists, whether certain religious beliefs are valid, or whether one religion is better than another. Sociologists cannot study such questions because they adhere to the scientific method, which requires them to study only observable and verifiable phenomena. Instead, they investigate the social aspects of religion, focusing on the characteristics common to all religions, the types of religious organizations, the functions and dysfunctions of religion, the conflicts within and between religious groups, the way in which religion shapes people's behavior and their understanding of the world, and the way in which religion is intertwined with social, economic, and political issues.

Here we begin with a definition of religion. Defining religion is a surprisingly difficult task and one with which sociologists have been greatly preoccupied.

What Is Religion? Weber's and Durkheim's Views

Figure 2 shows the "major religions" of the world. But what makes something a religion? In the opening sentences of *The Sociology of Religion*, Max Weber (1922) states, "To define 'religion,' to say what it is, is not possible at the start of a presentation such as this. Definition can be attempted, if at all, only at the conclusion of the study" (p. 1). Despite Weber's keen interest and his extensive writings about religious activity, he could offer only the broadest of definitions: religion encompasses those human responses that give meaning to the ultimate and inescapable problems of existence -birth, death, illness, aging, injustice, tragedy, and suffering (Abercrombie and Turner 1978). To Weber, the hundreds of thousands of religions, past and present, represented a rich and seemingly endless variety of responses to these problems. In view of this variety, he believed that no single definition could hope to capture the essence of religion.

Figure 2 Major Religions of the World
The map shows where certain large religious groups predominate around the world. There is much overlap, however—for example, millions of Catholics in the United States, millions of Muslims in India, many Protestants in Latin America. Other distinct religions do not appear on the map because they do not dominate a single large geographic area-for example, Judaism, Sikhism, Zoroastrianism (the Parsis). The term syncretismrefers to compatible combinations of belief systems, such as Confuciánism, Buddhism, Taoism, and Shinto in China and Japan (see "The World's Major Non-Christian Religions" later).

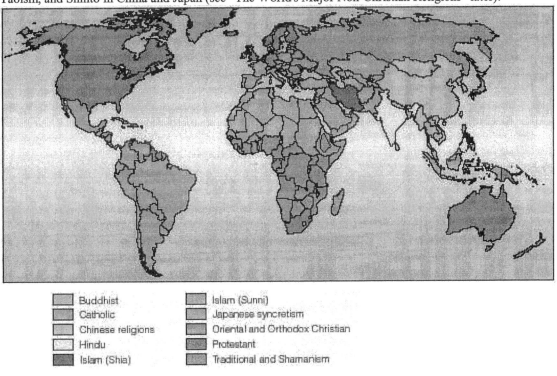

Buddhist		Islam (Sunni)	
Catholic		Japanese syncretism	
Chinese religions		Oriental and Orthodox Christian	
Hindu		Protestant	
Islam (Shia)		Traditional and Shamanism	

Like Max Weber, Emile Durkheim believed that nothing is as vague and diffused as religion. In the first chapter of his book *The Elementary Forms of the Religious Life*, Durkheim ([1915] 1964) cautions that when studying religions, sociologists must assume that "there are no religions which are false." Like Weber, Durkheim believed that all religions are true in their own fashion—all address the problems of human existence, albeit in different ways. Consequently, he said, those who study religion must first rid themselves of all preconceived notions of what religion should be. We cannot attribute to religion the characteristics that reflect only our own personal experiences and preferences.

In *The Spiritual Life of Children*, psychiatrist Robert Coles (1990) recounts his conversation with a 10-year-old Hopi girl, which illustrates Durkheim's point. The conversation reminds us that if we approach the study of religion with preconceived notions, we will lose many insights about the nature of religion in general:

> "The sky watches us and listens to us. It talks to us, and it hopes we are ready to talk back. The sky is where the God of the Anglos lives, a teacher told us. She [the teacher] asked where our God lives. I said, I don't know. I was telling the Truth! Our God is the sky, and lives wherever the sky is. Our God is the sun and the moon, too; and our God is our [the Hopi] people, if we remember to stay here [on the consecrated land]. This is where we're supposed to be, and if we leave, we lose God." [The interviewer then asked the child whether she had explained all of this to the teacher.]
>
> "No."
>
> "Why?"
>
> "Because — she thinks God is a person. If I'd told her, she'd give us that smile."
>
> "What smile?"
>
> "The smile that says to us, you kids are cute, but you're dumb; you're different—and you're all wrong!"
>
> "Perhaps you could have explained to her what you've just tried to explain to me."
>
> "We tried that a long time ago; our people spoke to the Anglos and told them what we think, but they don't listen to hear us; they listen to hear themselves." (p. 25)

Consider as a second example that many critics view the *hijab*, or modest dress of Muslim women, as evidence that the women are severely oppressed. Although women in the Middle East certainly do not have the same rights as men, critics should not be so quick to assume that the hijab is the source of oppression, especially when we consider the view that some Muslim women hold toward American dress customs:

> If women living in western societies took an honest look at themselves, such a question [as to why Muslim women are covered] would not arise. They are the slaves of appearance and the puppets of male chauvinistic society. Every magazine and news medium (such as television and radio) tells them how they should look and behave. They should wear glamorous clothes and make themselves beautiful for strange men to gaze and gloat over them.
>
> So the question is not why Muslim women wear *hijab*, but why the women in the West, who think they are so liberated, do not wear *hijab*? (Mahjubah 1984)

The conversation between Cole and the Hopi child and the discussion of hijab show that preconceived notions of what constitutes religion and uninformed opinions about the meaning of religious symbols and practices can close people off to a wide range of religious beliefs and experiences.

In formulating his ideas about religion, Durkheim remained open to the many varieties of religious experiences throughout the world. He identified three essential features that he believed were common to all religions, past and present: (1) beliefs about the sacred and the profane, (2) rituals, and (3) a community of worshipers. Thus Durkheim defined religion as a system of shared rituals and beliefs about the sacred that bind together a community of worshipers.

Beliefs About the Sacred and the Profane

At the heart of all religious belief and activity stands a distinction between two separate and opposing domains: the *sacred* and the profane. The sacred includes everything that is regarded as extraordinary and that inspires in believers deep and absorbing sentiments of awe, respect, mystery, and reverence. These sentiments motivate people to safeguard what is sacred from contamination or defilement. To find, preserve, or guard that which they consider sacred, people have gone to war, sacrificed their lives, traveled thousands of miles, and performed other life-endangering acts (Turner 1978).

Definitions of what is sacred vary according to time and place. Sacred things may include objects (chalices, sacred documents, and books), living creatures (cows, ants, birds), elements of nature (rocks, mountains, trees, the sea, sun, moon, or sky), places (churches, mosques, synagogues, birthplaces of religious founders), days that commemorate holy events, abstract forces (spirits, good, evil), persons (Christ, Buddha, Moses, Mohammed, Zarathustra, Nanak), states of consciousness (wisdom, oneness with nature), past events (the crucifixion, the resurrection, the escape of the Jews from Egypt, the birth of Buddha), ceremonies (baptism, marriage, burial), and other activities (holy wars, just wars, confession, fasting, pilgrimages).

Durkheim ([1915] 1964) maintains that the sacredness springs not from the item, ritual, or event itself, but rather from its symbolic power and from the emotions that people experience when they think about the sacred thing or when they are in its presence. These emotions are so strong that believers feel part of something larger than themselves and become outraged when others behave inappropriately in the presence of the sacred thing.

Ideas about what is sacred are such an important element of religious activity that many researchers classify religions according to the type of phenomenon that their followers consider sacred. One such typology consists of three categories: sacramental, prophetic, and mystical religions (Alston 1972).

In *sacramental religions*, followers seek the sacred in places, objects, and actions believed to house a god or a spirit. These locations may include inanimate objects (relics, statues, crosses), animals, trees, plants, foods, drink (wine, water), places, and certain processes (such as the way in which people prepare for a hunt or perform a dance). Examples of a sacramental religion include the various forms of Native Spirituality. An excerpt from the "Statement of Walter Echo-Hawk Before the United States Commission on Civil Rights" illustrates the sacramental qualities:

> First, I should tell you something about traditional or tribal religion, as native religion is vastly different from the Judeo-Christian religions most of us are familiar with. Because native religions are so different, the religion of the "redman" has never been understood by the non-Indian soldiers, missionaries, or government officials. (1) It is important to note that there are probably as many native religions as there are Indian tribes in this country. (2) None of these religions or religious tenets [has] been reduced to writing in a holy document such as the Bible or Koran.1 (3) None of these religions have man-made churches in the Judeo-Christian sense; rather the native religions are practiced in nature, at sacred sites, or in temporary religious structures—such as a tepee or sweat lodge. (4) The religious beliefs are tied to nature, the spiritual forces of nature, the natural elements, and the plants and creatures, which make up the environment. . . . Natives are dependent upon all these things in order to practice their many religious ceremonies, rituals and religious observances. (Echo-Hawk 1979:280)

In *prophetic religions*, the sacred revolves around items that symbolize significant historical events or around the lives, teachings, and writings of great people. Sacred books, such as the Christian Bible, the Muslim Koran, and the Jewish Torah hold the records of these events and revelations. In the case of historical events, God or some other higher being is believed to be directly involved in the course and the outcome of the event (a flood, the parting of the Red Sea, the rise and fall of an empire). In the case of great people, the lives and inspired words of prophets or messengers reveal a higher state of being, "the way," a set of ethical principles, or a code of conduct. Followers seek to imitate this life. Some of the best-known prophetic religions include Judaism as revealed to Abraham in Canaan and to Moses at Mount Sinai, Confucianism (founded by Confucius), Christianity (founded by Jesus Christ), and Islam (founded by Mohammed). The set of ethical principles may include "the Ten Commandments" or "the five pillars of Islam." Some of the later tenets are as follows:

- The declaration of faith known as the *Shahadah* (there is no god but Allah and Muhammad is his messenger)
- Obligatory prayer known as *salah* (prayer is performed five times a day)
- Alms giving (each year devout Muslims set aside a percentage of their accumulated wealth to assist the poor and sick)
- A pilgrimage to Mecca, known as *Haij* (the person must be physically and financially able to make the pilgrimage to Mecca)

In *mystical religions*, followers seek the sacred in states of being that, at their peak, can exclude all awareness of one's existence, sensations, thoughts, and surroundings. In such states, the mystic becomes caught up so fully in the transcendental experience that earthly concerns seem to vanish. Direct union with the divine forces of the universe assumes the utmost importance. Not surprisingly, mystics tend to become involved in practices such as fasting or celibacy to separate themselves from worldly attachments. In addition, they meditate to clear their minds of worldly concern, "leaving the soul empty and receptive to influences from the divine" (Alston 1972:144). Buddhism and philosophical Hinduism are two examples of religions that emphasize physical and spiritual discipline as a means of transcending the self and earthly concerns.

Keep in mind that the distinctions among sacramental, prophetic, and mystical religions are not clearcut. In fact, most religions incorporate or combine elements of other religions. Consequently, the majority of religions cannot be classified into a single category, although one category often predominates.

According to Durkheim ([1915] 1964), the sacred encompasses more than the forces of good: "There are gods [that is, satans] of theft and trickery, of lust and war, of sickness and of death" (p. 420). Evil and its various representations, however, are generally portrayed as inferior and subordinate to the forces of good: "in the majority of cases we see the good victorious over evil, life over death, the powers of light over the powers of darkness" (p. 421). Even so, Durkheim considers superordinary evil phenomena to fall under the category "sacred" (as he defines it) because they are endowed with special powers and serve as the object of rituals (confessions, baptisms, penance, fasting, exorcism) designed to overcome or resist their negative influences.

Religious beliefs, doctrines, legends, and myths detail the origins, virtues, and powers of sacred things and describe the consequences of mixing the sacred with the profane. The *profane* encompasses everything that is not sacred, including things opposed to the sacred (the unholy, the irreverent, the contemptuous, the blasphemous) and things that stand apart from the sacred, although not in opposition to it (the ordinary, the commonplace, the unconsecrated, the temporal, the bodily) (Ebersole 1967). Believers often view contact between the sacred and the profane as being dangerous and sacrilegious, as threatening the very existence of the sacred, and as endangering the fate of the person who made or allowed the contact. Consequently, people take action to safeguard sacred things by separating them in some way from the profane. For example, some people refrain from speaking the name of God in frustration; others believe that a woman must cover her hair or her face during worship and that a man must remove his hat during worship.

The distinctions between the sacred and the profane do not mean that a person, object, or idea cannot pass from one domain to another or that something profane cannot ever come into contact with the sacred. Such transformations and contacts are authorized through rituals—the active and most observable side of religion.

Rituals

In the religious sense, *rituals* are rules that govern how people must behave in the presence of the sacred to achieve an acceptable state of being. These rules may take the form of instructions detailing the appropriate context for worship, the roles of various participants, acceptable dress, and the precise wording of chants, songs, and prayers. Participants must follow instructions closely so as to achieve a specific goal, whether it be to purify the participant's body or soul (confession, immersion, fasting, seclusion), to commemorate an important person or event (pilgrimage to Mecca, Passover, the Last Supper), or to transform profane items into sacred items (water to holy water, bones to sacred relics). During rituals, behavior is "coordinated to an inner intention to make contact with, or to participate in, the invisible world or to achieve a desired state" (Smart 1976, p. 6).

Rituals can be as simple as closing one's eyes to pray or having one's forehead be marked with ashes; they can also be as elaborate as fasting for three days before entering a sacred place to chant, with head bowed, a particular prayer for forgiveness. Although rituals are often enacted in sacred places, some are codes of conduct aimed at governing the performance of everyday activities—sleeping, walking, eating, defecating, washing, dealing with the opposite sex.

The Taliban has received worldwide attention for the code of conduct that it imposed on those under its rule and for the severe punishments issued to those who violated these codes. For example, the Taliban mandated that women who appear in public must be covered from head to toe; they were not permitted to leave their homes without an acceptable reason or to work outside the home even as health care workers or as distributors of international aid. Members of the Taliban sought out and destroyed things they considered un-Islamic, including tape recorders, cassettes, toys, TVs, and car radio antennas (Amnesty International 1996a, 1996b).

According to Durkheim, the nature of the ritual is relatively insignificant. Rather, the important element is that the ritual be shared by a community or worshipers and evoke certain ideas and sentiments that help individuals feel part of something bigger than themselves.

Community of Worshipers

Durkheim uses the word church to designate a group whose members hold the same beliefs with regard to the sacred and the profane, who behave in the same way in the presence of the sacred, and who gather in body or spirit at agreed-on times to reaffirm their commitment to those beliefs and practices. Obviously, religious beliefs and practices cannot be unique to an individual; they must be shared by a group of people. If not, then the beliefs and practices would cease to exist when the individual who held them died or if he or she chose to abandon them. In the social sense, religion is inseparable from the idea of church. The gathering and the sharing create a moral community and allow worshipers to share a common identity. The gathering, however, need not take place in a common setting. When people perform a ritual on a given day or at given times of day, the gathering is spiritual rather than physical.

Durkheim ([1915] 1964) uses the term "church" loosely, acknowledging that it can assume many forms: "Sometimes it embraces an entire people . . . sometimes it embraces only a part of them . . . sometimes it is directed by a corps of priests, sometimes it is almost completely devoid of any official directing body" (p. 44). Sociologists have identified at least five broad types of religious organizations (communities of worshipers): ecclesiae, denominations, sects, established sects, and cults. As with most classification schemes, the categories overlap on some characteristics because the classification criteria for religions are not always clear.

ECCLESIAE   An *ecclesiae* is a professionally trained religious organization governed by a hierarchy of leaders, which claims everyone in a society as its members. Membership is not voluntary; it is the law. Consequently, considerable political alignment exists between church and state officials, so that the ecclesiae represents the official church of the state. Ecclesiae formerly existed in England (the Anglican church), France (the Roman Catholic church), and Sweden (the Lutheran church). The 1987 Afghanistan constitution stated that the religion of Afghanistan is Islam. Today Islam is the official religion of Bangladesh and Malaysia, Iran has been an Islamic republic since the Ayatollah Khomeini took power in 1979, and Saudi Arabia is a monarchy based on Islamic law (*World Almanac and Book of Facts* 2001).

Individuals are born into ecclesiae; newcomers to the society are converted; dissenters often are persecuted. Those who do not accept the official view tend to emigrate or occupy the most marginal status in the society. The ecclesiae claims to be the one true faith and often does not recognize other religions as valid. In its most extreme form, it directly controls all facets of life. In Afghanistan, for example, non-Muslims must conform to Islamic legal and unwritten restrictions and are prohibited from proselytizing (Kurian 1992).

DENOMINATIONS   A *denomination* is a hierarchical organization in a society in which church and state usually remain separate; it is led by a professionally trained clergy. In contrast to an ecclesiae, a denomination is one of many religious organizations in the society. For the most part, denominations tolerate other religious organizations; they may even collaborate to address and solve some problems in the society. Although membership is considered to be voluntary, most people who belong to denominations did not choose to join them. Rather, they were born to parents who are members. Denominational leaders generally make few demands on the laity, and most members participate in limited and specialized ways. For example, they may choose to send their children to church-operated schools, attend church on Sundays and religious holidays, donate money, or attend church-sponsored functions. The leaders of a denomination do not oversee all aspects of the members' lives. Yet, even though laypeople vary widely in lifestyle, denominations frequently attract people of particular races and social classes— that is, their members are drawn disproportionately from specific social and ethnic groups.

Eight major religious denominations exist in the world—Buddhism, Christianity, Confucianism, Hinduism, Islam, Judaism, Taoism, and Shinto—each dominant in different areas of the globe (see "The World's Major Non-Christian Religions" in this excerpt). For example, Christianity predominates in Europe, North and South America, New Zealand, Australia, and the Pacific Islands; Islam predominates in the Middle East and North Africa; Hinduism predominates in India.

SECTS AND ESTABLISHED SECTS   A *sect* is a small community of believers led by a lay ministry, with no formal hierarchy or official governing body to oversee the various religious gatherings and activities. Sects typically are composed of people who broke away from a denomination because they came to view it as corrupt. They then created the offshoot in an effort to reform the religion from which they separated.

All of the major religions encompass splinter groups that have sought, at one time or another, to preserve the integrity of their religion. In Islam, for example, the most pronounced split occurred 1,300 years ago, approximately 30 years after the death of the Prophet Mohammed. The dividing issue related to Mohammed's successor. The Shia maintained that the successor should be a blood relative of Mohammed; the Sunni believed that the successor should be selected by the community of believers and need not be related by blood. After Mohammed's death, the Sunni (encompassing the great majority of Muslims) accepted Abu-Bakr as the caliph (successor). The Shia supported Ali, Mohammad's first cousin and son-inlaw, and they called for the overthrow of the existing order and a return to the pure form of Islam. Today Shiaism represents the dominant religion in the Islamic Republic of Iran (95 percent), and Sunni Muslim dominates in the Islamic Republics of Pakistan (77 percent) and Afghanistan (84 percent).

The divisions within Islam have existed for so long that Sunni and Shia have become recognized as *established sects*, renegades from denominations or ecclesiae that have existed long enough to acquire a large following and widespread respectability. In some ways, established sects resemble both denominations and sects. As you might expect, several divisions exist within each established sect, as splinter groups attempted to reform some policy, practice, or position held by the religious organization from which they separated.

Similarly, several splits have occurred within the Christian churches. In 1054, for example, the Eastern Orthodox churches rejected the pope as the earthly deputy of Christ and questioned the papal claim of authority over all Catholic churches in the world. The Protestant religions owe their origins to Martin Luther (1483–1546), who also challenged the papal authority and protested many of the practices of the Roman Catholic church.[1] Divisions also exist within various Protestant sects and between Catholics. Offshoots of the Roman Catholic Church, for example, include Maronites, Greek Catholics, Greek Orthodox, Jacobites, and Gregorians.

[1]This protest was dubbed the Reformation because it involved efforts to reform the Catholic church and to cleanse it of corruption, especially with regard to paying for indulgences (the forgiveness of sins upon saying specific prayers or performing specific good deeds at the order of a priest). Luther believed that a person is saved not by the intercession of priests or bishops, but by private and individual faith (Van Doren 1991).

People are not born into sects, as they are with denominations; theoretically, they convert. Consequently, newborns are not baptized; they choose membership later in life, when they are considered able to decide for themselves. Sects vary on many levels, including the degree to which they view society as religiously bankrupt or corrupt and the extent to which they take action to change people in society.

CULTS   Generally, *cults* are very small, loosely organized groups, usually founded by a charismatic leader who attracts people by virtue of his or her personal qualities. Because the charismatic leader plays such a central role in attracting members, cults often dissolve after the leader dies. For this reason, few cults last long enough to become established religions. Even so, a few manage to survive, as evidenced by the fact that the major world religions began as cults.

Because cults form around new and unconventional religious practices, outsiders tend to view them with considerable suspicion.

Cults vary according to their purpose and to the level of commitment that the cult leaders demand of converts. They may draw members by focusing on highly specific, but eccentric interests, such as astrology, UFOs, or transcendental meditation. Members may be attracted by the promise of companionship, a cure from illness, relief from suffering, or enlightenment. A cult may meet infrequently and strictly voluntarily (such as at conventions or monthly meetings). In some cases, however, the cult leaders may require members to break all ties with family, friends, and jobs and thus to come to rely exclusively on the cult to meet all their needs.

A Critique of Durkheim's Definition of Religion

Durkheim's definition of religion relies on the most outward, most visible characteristics of religion. Critics argue, however, that the three essential characteristics—beliefs about the sacred and the profane, rituals, and a community of worshipers—are not unique to religious activity. This combination of characteristics, they say, applies to many gatherings—sporting events, graduation ceremonies, reunions, and political rallies—and many political systems (for example, Marxism, Maoism, and fascism). On the basis of these characteristics alone, it is difficult to distinguish between an assembly of Christians celebrating Christmas, a patriotic group supporting the initiation of a war against another country, and a group of fans eulogizing James Dean or Elvis Presley. In other words, religion is not the only unifying force in society that incorporates these three elements defined by Durkheim as characteristic of religion. Civil religion represents another such force that resembles religion as Durkheim defined it.

The World's Major Non-Christian Religions

BUDDHISM
Buddhism has 307 million followers. It was founded by Siddhartha Gautama, known as the Buddha (Enlightened One), in southern Nepal in the sixth and fifth centuries B.C. The Buddha achieved enlightenment through meditation and gathered a community of monks to carry on his teachings. Buddhism teaches that meditation and the practice of good religious and moral behavior can lead to Nirvana, the state of enlightenment, although before achieving Nirvana one is subject to repeated lifetimes that are good or bad depending on one's actions (karma). The doctrines of the Buddha describe temporal life as featuring "four noble truths": existence is a realm of suffering; desire, along with the belief in the importance of one's self, causes suffering; achievement of Nirvana ends suffering; and Nirvana is attained only by meditation and by following the path of righteousness in action, thought, and attitude.

CONFUCIANISM
A faith with 5.6 million followers, Confucianism was founded by Confucius, a Chinese philosopher, in the sixth and fifth centuries B.C. Confucius's sayings and dialogues, known collectively as the Analects, were written down by his followers. Confucianism, which grew out of a strife-ridden time in Chinese history, stresses the relationship between individuals, their families, and society, based on li (proper behavior) and jen (sympathetic attitude). Its practical, socially oriented philosophy was challenged by the more mystical precepts of Taoism and Buddhism, which were partially incorporated to create neo-Confucianism during the Sung dynasty (A.D. 960–1279). The overthrow of the Chinese monarchy and the Communist revolution during the twentieth century have severely lessened the influence of Confucianism on modern Chinese culture.

HINDUISM

A religion with 648 million followers, Hinduism developed from indigenous religions of India in combination with Aryan religions brought to India in c. 1500 B.C. and codified in the Veda and the Upanishads, the sacred scriptures of Hinduism. Hinduism is a term used to broadly describe a vast array of sects to which most Indians belong. Although many Hindu reject the caste system—in which people are born into a particular subgroup that determines their religious, social, and work-related duties—it is widely accepted and classifies society at large into four groups: the Brahmins or priests, the rulers and warriors, the farmers and merchants, and the peasants and laborers. The goals of Hinduism are release from repeated reincarnation through the practice of yoga, adherence to Vedic scriptures, and devotion to a personal guru. Various deities are worshiped at shrines; the divine trinity, representing the cyclical nature of the universe, are Brahma the creator, Vishnu the preserver, and Shiva the destroyer.

ISLAM

Islam has 840 million followers. It was founded by the prophet Muhammad, who received the holy scriptures of Islam, the Koran, from Allah (God) c. A.D. 610. Islam (Arabic for "submission to God") maintains that Muhammad is the last in a long line of holy prophets, preceded by Adam, Abraham, Moses, and Jesus. In addition to being devoted to the Koran, followers of Islam (Muslims) are devoted to the worship of Allah through the Five Pillars: the statement "There is no god but God, and Muhammad is his prophet"; prayer, conducted five times a day while facing Mecca; the giving of alms; the keeping of the fast of Ramadan during the ninth month of the Muslim year; and the making of a pilgrimage at least once to Mecca, if possible. The two main divisions of Islam are the Sunni and the Shiite; the Wahabis are the most important Sunni sect, while the Shiite sects include the Assassins, the Druses, and the Fatimids, among countless others.

JUDAISM

Stemming from the descendants of Judah in Judea, Judaism was founded c. 2000 B.C. by Abraham, Isaac, and Jacob and has 18 million followers. Judaism espouses belief in a monotheistic God, who is creator of the universe and who leads His people, the Jews, by speaking through prophets. His word is revealed in the Hebrew Bible (or Old Testament), especially in that part known as the Torah. The Torah also contains, according to Rabbinic tradition, a total of 613 biblical commandments, including the Ten Commandments, which are explicated in the Talmud. Jews believe that the human condition can be improved, that the letter and the spirit of the Torah must be followed, and that a Messiah will eventually bring the world to a state of paradise. Judaism promotes community among all people of Jewish faith, dedication to a synagogue or temple (the basic social unit of a group of Jews, led by a rabbi), and the importance of family life. Religious observance takes place both at home and in temple. Judaism is divided into three main groups who vary in their interpretation of those parts of the Torah that deal with personal, communal, international, and religious activities: the Orthodox community, which views the Torah as derived from God, and therefore absolutely binding; the Reform movement, which follows primarily its ethical content; and the Conservative Jews, who follow most of the observances set out in the Torah but allow for change in the face of modern life. A fourth group, reconstructionist Jews, rejects the concept of the Jews as God's chosen people, yet maintains rituals as part of the Judaic cultural heritage.

SHINTO

Shinto, with 3.5 million followers, is the ancient native religion of Japan, established long before the introduction of writing to Japan in the fifth century A.D. The origins of its beliefs and rituals are unknown. Shinto stresses belief in a great many spiritual beings and gods, known as kami, who are paid tribute at shrines and honored by festivals, and reverence for ancestors. While there is no overall dogma, adherents of Shinto are expected to remember and celebrate the kami, support the societies of which the kami are patrons, remain pure and sincere, and enjoy life.

TAOISM

Both a philosophy and a religion, Taoism was founded in China by Lao-tzu, who is traditionally said to have been born in 604 B.C. Its number of followers is uncertain. It derives primarily from the Tao-teching, which claims that an ever-changing universe follows the Tao, or path. The Tao can be known only by emulating its quietude and effortless simplicity; Taoism prescribes that people live simply, spontaneously, and in close touch with nature and that they meditate to achieve contact with the Tao. Temples and monasteries, maintained by Taoist priests, are important in some Taoist sects. Since the Communist revolution, Taoism has been actively discouraged in the People's Republic of China, although it continues to flourish in Taiwan.

Look back at several of these descriptions. What are some sacramental, prophetic, and mystical characteristics they mention? Suppose you were asked to write a brief piece describing Christianity in the same ways that the other major religions are described here. What would you say?

Source: Reprinted with permission of Macmillan General Reference USA, a Simon & Schuster Macmillan Company, from The New York Public Library Desk Reference, second edition. A Stonesong Press book. Copyright © 1989, 1993 by The New York Public Library and The Stonesong Press, Inc. The name, "The New York Public Library," is a trademark and the property of The New York Public Library, Astor, Lenox, and Tilden Foundations.

Civil Religion

Civil religion is "any set of beliefs and rituals, related to the past, present and/or future of a people (nation), which are understood in some transcendental fashion" (Hammond 1976, p. 171). A nation's beliefs (such as individual freedom or equal opportunity) and rituals (parades, fireworks, singing of the national anthem, 21-gun salutes, and so on) often assume a sacred quality. Even in the face of internal divisions based on race, ethnicity, region, religion, or gender, national beliefs and rituals can still inspire awe, respect, and reverence for the country. These sentiments are most notably evident on national holidays that celebrate important events or people (such as Presidents' Day, Martin Luther King Jr. Day, or Independence Day), in the presence of national monuments or symbols (the flag, the Capitol, the Lincoln Memorial, the Vietnam Memorial, etc.), and at times of war or other national crises such as war.

The Cold War

During the Cold War, relations with the Soviet Union fell short of direct, full-scale military engagement; even so, as many as 120 proxy wars were fought in developing countries. In many of these conflicts, the United States and the Soviet Union supported opposing factions with weapons and other military equipment, combat training, medical supplies, economic aid, and food. Three of the best-known proxy wars were fought in Korea, Vietnam, and Afghanistan.

Soviet and American leaders justified their direct or indirect intervention in these proxy wars on the grounds that it was necessary to contain the spread of the other side's economic and political system, to protect national and global security, and to prevent the other side from shifting the balance of power in favor of its system.

Americans and Muslims as Cold War Partners

Afghanistan is landlocked, and two-thirds of its terrain is mountainous. China, Iran, Pakistan, and three former Soviet republics (Tajikistan, Turkmenistan, and Uzbekistan) border the country. Given its location, it is not surprising that many foreign governments showed great interest in Afghanistan. Consequently, the factional fighting in Afghanistan has been backed by foreign powers.

The Cold War between the United States and the Soviet Union made Afghanistan a focus of those two countries' conflict. When the Soviet Union invaded Afghanistan in 1979 and put its Afghan supporters in charge, the United States supported the Afghan freedom fighters, known as the *mujahidin*, by funneling money through Pakistan. At that time, Pakistani President Zia's goal was to turn Pakistan into the leader of the Islamic world and then use that leverage to cultivate an Islamic opposition to Soviet expansion into Central Asia. Zia's aims fit well with the U.S. Cold War goals of containing the Soviet Union. If the U.S. could show the Soviet Union that the entire Muslim world was its partner, then the U.S. would indeed be a force to fear (Rashid 2001).

The U.S. CIA worked with Pakistan's Inter-Services Intelligence Agency (the equivalent of the CIA) on a plan to recruit radical Muslims from all over the world to fight with their Afghan brothers against the Soviet Union. An estimated 35,000 Muslims from 43 countries—primarily in Central Asia, North and East Africa, and the Middle East—heeded the call. Thousands more came to Pakistan to study in *madrassas* (religious schools) located in Pakistan and along the Afghan border (Rashid 2001).

Military training camps staffed with the U.S. advisors helped train guerilla fighters, and the *madrassas* offered a place for the most radical Muslims in the world to meet, exchange ideas, and learn about Islamic movements in one another's countries. Among those who came to Afghanistan was Osama bin Laden. At that time, the pressing question for the U.S. as asked by national security advisor Zbigniew Brzezinski (2001) was "What was more important in the world view of history? The possible creation of an armed, radical Islamic movement or the fall of the Soviet Empire? A few fired-up Muslims or the liberation of Central Europe and the end of the Cold War?"

These Pakistan-U.S.-supported recruiting and military centers would eventually evolve into al-Qaida ("the base"). In 1989, the year the term "al-Qaida" was first used, Osama bin Laden had taken over as the centers' leader. That same year, the Soviets withdrew from Afghanistan, leaving behind

> an uneasy coalition of Islamic organizations intent on promoting Islam among all non-Muslim forces. It left behind a legacy of expert and experienced fighters, training camps and logistical facilities, elaborate trans-Islam networks of personal and organizational relationships, a substantial amount of military equipment. . . and most importantly, a heavy sense of power and self-confidence based on what it had achieved, and a driving desire to move on to other victories (Huntington 2001, p. A12)

This brief overview of the Cold War has shown that the economic and political beliefs of the Soviet Union and the United States assumed a sacred quality that unified and motivated each side to sacrifice millions of human lives at home and abroad in the name of those principles. The larger point is that the traits cited by Durkheim as characteristics of religion apply to other events, relationships, and forces within society that many people might not define as religious.

47

One might argue that if Durkheim's definition of religion allows us to equate the Soviet and American roles in the Cold War with an Islamic response, then perhaps sociologists should develop a narrower, less inclusive definition of religion than that proposed by Durkheim. Narrow definitions are problematic as well, however. Suppose that we narrow the definition of religion to "the belief in an ever-living god." This definition would exclude polytheistic religions such as Hinduism, which has more than 640 million adherents. It would also exclude religions in which a deity plays little or no role, such as Buddhism, which has more than 300 million followers. As you can see, narrow definitions of religion offer no improvement relative to broad ones.

Despite its shortcomings, Durkheim's definition of religion remains one of the best and most widely used. No sociologist with any standing in the discipline can study religion without encountering and addressing Durkheim's definition. The question "What is religion?" is not just a sociological question, but also a question asked by those governments that guarantee their residents freedom of religion.

Two Opposing Trends: Secularization and Fundamentalism

Secularization and fundamentalism are processes that have become increasingly popular in the recent past. Each has expanded in spite of the other's growth, or possibly in opposition to it.

Secularization

In the most general sense, *secularization* is a process by which religious influences on thought and behavior are reduced. It is difficult to generalize about the causes and consequences of secularization because they vary across contexts. Americans and Europeans associate secularization with an increase in scientific understanding and technological solutions to everyday problems of living. In effect, science and technology assume roles that were once filled by religious belief and practice. Most Muslims, in contrast, do not attribute secularization to science or to modernization; indeed, many devout Muslims are physical scientists.

From a Muslim perspective, secularization is a Western-imposed phenomenon—specifically, a result of exposure to what many people in the Middle East consider the most negative of Western values.

Subjective secularization is a decrease in the number of people who view the world and their place in it from a religious perspective. In other words, paradigms shift from a religious understanding of the world grounded in faith, to an understanding grounded in observable evidence and the scientific method. In the face of uncertainty, secular thinkers do not turn to religion or to a supernatural power that they have come to view as a distant, impersonal, and even inactive phenomenon. Consequently, they come to believe less in direct intervention by the supernatural and to rely more strongly on human intervention or scientific explanation.

Considerable debate exists over the extent to which secularization is taking place. Data collected by the Gallup Organization over the past 25 years show little change in the degree of importance that Americans assign to religion. More than 90 percent have a religious preference, and almost 70 percent are members of one of the more than 250,000 places of worship in the United States (White House press release 1995); approximately 30 percent attend church weekly; and almost 60 percent state that religion is very important in their lives (the Gallup Organization 2001). Polls also show that almost 80 percent of Americans are "sometimes very conscious of God's presence" and that more than 80 percent agree that "even today, miracles are performed by the power of God" (Gallup and Castelli 1989, p. 58).

Fundamentalism

In "Popular Conceptions of Fundamentalism," anthropologist Lionel Caplan (1987) offers his readers an extremely clear overview of a complex religious phenomenon—fundamentalism, a belief in the timeless nature of sacred writings and a belief that such writings apply to all kinds of environments. In its popular usage, this term is applied to a wide array of religious groups in the United States and around the world, including the Moral Majority in the United States, Orthodox Jews in Israel, and various Islamic groups in the Middle East.

Religious groups labeled as fundamentalist are usually portrayed as "fossilized relics . . . living perpetually in a bygone age" (Caplan 1987:5). Americans frequently employ this simplistic analysis to explain events in the Middle East, especially the causes of the political turmoil that threatens the interests of the United States (including its need for oil). Such oversimplification misrepresents fundamentalism, however, and it cannot explain the widespread appeal of contemporary fundamentalist movements within several of the world's religions.

THE COMPLEXITY OF FUNDAMENTALISM   Fundamentalism is a more complex phenomenon than popular conceptions lead us to believe. It is impossible to define a fundamentalist in terms of age, ethnicity, social class, or political ideology, because fundamentalism appeals to a wide range of people. Moreover, fundamentalist groups do not always position themselves against those in power; in fact, they are equally likely to be neutral or to support existing regimes fervently. Perhaps the most important characteristic of fundamentalists is their belief that a relationship with God, Allah, or some other supernatural force provides answers to personal and social problems. In addition, fundamentalists often wish to "bring the wider culture back to its religious roots" (Lechner 1989:51).

Caplan (1987) identifies a number of other traits that seem to characterize fundamentalists. First, fundamentalists emphasize the authority, infallibility, and timeless truth of sacred writings as a "definitive blueprint" for life (p. 19). This characteristic does not mean that any definitive interpretation of sacred writings actually exists. Any sacred text has as many interpretations as there are groups that claim it as their blueprint. For example, even members of the same fundamentalist organization may disagree about the true meaning of the texts they follow.

Second, fundamentalists usually conceive of history as a "process of decline from an original ideal state, [and] hardly more than a catalog of the betrayal of fundamental principles" (p. 18). They conceptualize human history as a "cosmic struggle between good and evil:" the good results from one's dedication to principles outlined in sacred scriptures, and the evil is an outcome of countless digressions from sacred principles. To fundamentalists, truth is not a relative phenomenon; it does not vary across time and place. Instead, truth is unchanging and knowable through the sacred texts.

Third, fundamentalists do not distinguish between the sacred and the profane in their day-to-day lives. Religious principles govern all areas of life, including family, business, and leisure. Religious behavior, in their view, does not take place only in a church, a mosque, or a temple.

Fourth, fundamentalist religious groups emerge for a reason, usually in reaction to a perceived threat or crisis, whether real or imagined. Consequently, any discussion of a particular fundamentalist group must include some reference to an adversary.

Fifth, one obvious concern for fundamentalists is the need to reverse the trend toward gender equality, which they believe is symptomatic of a declining moral order. In fundamentalist religions, women's rights often become subordinated to ideals that the group considers more important to the well-being of the society, such as the traditional family or the right to life. Such a priority of ideals is regarded as the correct order of things.

ISLAMIC FUNDAMENTALISM   In *The Islamic Threat: Myth or Reality?* (1992), professor of religious studies John L.Esposito maintains that most Americans' understanding of fundamentalism does not apply very well to contemporary Islam. The term fundamentalism has its roots in American Protestantism and the twentieth-century movement that emphasizes the literal interpretation of the Bible. Fundamentalists are portrayed as static, literalist, retrogressive, and extremist. Just as we cannot apply the term fundamentalism to all Protestants in the United States, so too we cannot apply it to the entire Muslim world, especially when we consider that Muslims make up the majority of the population in at least 45 countries.

Esposito believes that a more apt term is *Islamic revitalism* or *Islamic activism*. The form of Islamic revitalism may vary from one country to another, but seems to be characterized by the following themes:

> A sense that existing political, economic, and social systems had failed; a disenchantment with and at times a rejection of the West; a quest for identity and greater authenticity; and the conviction that Islam provides a self-sufficient ideology for state and society, a valid alternative to secular nationalism, socialism, and capitalism. (Esposito 1992, p.14)

In "Islam in the Politics of the Middle East," Esposito (1986) asks, "Why has religion [specifically Islam] become such a visible force in Middle East politics?" He believes that Islamic revitalism represents a "response to the failures and crises of authority and legitimacy that have plagued most modern Muslim states" (p. 53). Recall that after World War I, France and Britain carved up the Middle East into nationstates, drawing the boundaries so as to meet the economic and political needs of Western powers. Lebanon, for example, was created in part to establish a Christian tie to the West; Israel was envisioned as a refuge for persecuted Jews when no country seemed to want them; the Kurds received no state; Iraq became virtually landlocked; and resource-rich territories were incorporated into states with very sparse populations (Kuwait, Saudi Arabia, the Emirates). Their citizens viewed many of the leaders who took control of these foreign creations "as autocratic heads of corrupt, authoritarian regimes that [were] propped up by Western governments and multinational corporations" (p. 54).

When Arab armies from six states lost "so quickly, completely, and publicly" to Israel in 1967, Arabs were forced to question the political and moral structure of their societies (Hourani 1991:442). Had the leaders and the people abandoned Islamic principles or deviated too far? Could a return to a stricter Islamic way of life restore confidence to the Middle East and give it an identity independent of the West? Questions of social justice also arose. Oil wealth and modernization policies had led to rapid increases in population and urbanization and opened up a vast chasm between the oil-rich countries, such as Kuwait and Saudi Arabia, and the poor, densely populated countries, such as Egypt, Pakistan, and Bangladesh. Western capitalism, which was seen as one of the primary forces behind these trends, seemed blind to social justice, instead promoting unbridled consumption and widespread poverty. Likewise, Marxist socialism (a godless alternative) had failed to produce social justice. It is no wonder that the Taliban and other Muslim groups in Afghanistan rejected Western capitalism and Marxist socialism because the disintegration of Afghanistan is a direct product of the Cold War between the United States and the former Soviet Union.

For many people, Islam offers an alternative vision for society. According to Esposito (1986), five beliefs guide Islamic activists (who follow many political persuasions, ranging from conservative to militant):
1. Islam is a comprehensive way of life relevant to politics, state, law, and society.
2. Muslim societies fail when they depart from Islamic ways and follow the secular and materialistic ways of the West.
3. An Islamic social and political revolution is necessary for renewal.
4. Islamic law must replace Western-inspired or Western-imposed laws.
5. Science and technology must be used in ways that reflect Islamic values to guard against the infiltration of Western values.

Muslim groups differ dramatically in their beliefs about how quickly and by what methods these principles should be implemented. Most Muslims, however, are willing to work within existing political arrangements; they condemn violence as a method of bringing about political and social change.

The information presented in this section points out the complex interplay of religion with political, economic, historical, and other social forces. Fundamentalism cannot be viewed in simple terms; rather, any analysis must consider the broader context. A focus on context allows us to see that fundamentalism can represent a reaction to many events and processes, including secularization, foreign influence, failure or crisis in authority, the loss of a homeland, and rapid change.

Part III: The Globalization Process and Terrorism from an Anthropological Perspective

The globalization process in recent years has sparked strong debate and outright confrontation, one example being the street demonstrations that occurred in Seattle and Genoa, Italy on the occasion of international trade and economic meetings. Garrick Bailey is an anthropologist from the University of Tulsa and the co-author of the cultural anthropology text Humanity: An Introduction to Cultural Anthropology, Sixth Edition *(2003). The following examines how anthropology can help us understand the forces at work in the globalization process and how these forces may contribute to the rise of terrorism.*

A. Globalization
This essay was obtained from James Peoples and Garrick Bailey, *Humanity: An Introduction to Cultural Anthropology*, Sixth Edition (Wadsworth, 2003).

Until the violent street protests at the meeting of the World Trade Organization at Seattle in late 1999, few Americans had given more than passing attention to issues of globalization and free trade. To most, globalization seemed to be part of the natural evolution of the world economic system, which during the decade of the 1990s had resulted in economic prosperity for the United States. We assumed that globalization was bringing or would eventually bring prosperity to the rest of the peoples of the world as well. Since Seattle, virtually every major international economic meeting or summit has brought increasing numbers of protesters into the streets. At the G-8 meetings in Genoa, Italy in the summer of 2001, between 100,000 and 150,000 demonstrators filled the streets. What the problem? The protestors have been variously labeled "anti-capitalists," "anarchists," "environmentalists," and even "Ludites." But no single label can readily be applied to these protesters since they range widely in their concerns about the effects of globalization and in their ideologies.

Globalization is not simply an economic issue. Globalization has far reaching political, social, and cultural implications for the world's peoples. In the proceeding chapters we have raised in boxes some of the more specific questions concerning globalization. In this chapter we are going to discuss the history of globalization together with some of its consequences.

It was not until the 1980s that the term *globalization* first came into common usage. Today, although we hear and use the term almost daily, we might find it difficult to define. Globalization is not a thing or a product, but rather a process. *Globalization* refers to the worldwide changes which are increasingly integrating and remolding the lives of the people of the world. Most commonly we speak of the global economy and think of globalization primarily in economic terms. Although economic changes are certainly the driving force behind globalization, it is having far more profound effects on our way of life than merely what we eat, what we wear, and how we make our living. It is having an impact on our political, social, and cultural institutions as well.

Globalization began 500 years ago, with the voyage of Columbus, and has had two stages of development. The earliest stage, the period from about 1500 to the mid-twentieth century, saw the development of a global trade network, which eventually connected, directly indirectly, almost every group of people in the world. The second stage, which began to develop at the end of World War II, saw the development of global marketing of products and the emergence of a global economy.

The Emergence of the Global Economy

Over the past fifty years the process of globalization has entered a new and different phase. A global economy has started to evolve. In its essence the global economy is simple: the creation of a global market and the integration of peoples and communities into this market. *Global trade* involved the exchange of goods between regional markets. In the *global economy* all labor, goods, and services are bought and sold on the global market.

We can readily see some effects of the global economy. The price we pay for a sack of flour in Kansas or a gallon of gasoline in Texas is already determined in large part by the world price for wheat and oil. Similarly the price we pay for a Ford is no longer solely influenced by competition from General Motors, but by oversea auto manufacturers as well. Foreign imports not only place American companies in competition with foreign companies, but also put American workers in direct competition with their foreign counterparts. American farmers, oil producers, businesspeople, and workers are now finding that they have to compete on a global market for the prices they can charge for their goods and labor. This has both good and bad points. It has resulted in cheaper prices in the United States for many manufactured goods. However, it has also meant the loss of jobs as companies, in order to compete, have closed their domestic manufacturing plants and laid off their relatively high-paid American workers, building new overseas plants staffed by low-paid foreign workers and importing the products back to the United States for sale. As a result many American companies are no longer producing the products they sell in the United States.

Many scholars argue that the global economy differs qualitatively from global trade in that implicit in the global economy is an underlying and unifying ideology, capitalism, and a single objective, the production of wealth. Capitalism is an ideology based on Western (European) cultural beliefs and values. For a people to survive, let alone prosper, in the new emerging global economy, they have to adopt Western cultural ideas. Thus the global economy is not merely resulting in the restructuring of the world economic system, but is having far-ranging cultural and social consequences for the peoples of the world as well.

The world today, at the being of the twenty-first century, is a far different place from what it was when your grandparents were young. The past fifty years have seen vast changes in the lives of virtually all of the peoples of the world. The Second World War was a major watershed in human history. As we have seen, before World War II the world economic system was dominated by European-controlled colonial empires. The British, French, and Soviet (or Russian) empires were the largest. However, the Netherlands, Belgium, Spain, Portugal and Italy also had overseas possessions. Even the United States had the Philippines, Guam, Samoa, and Puerto Rico. Global trade existed, but there was no integrated global economy. These empires had been created for only one reason: the economic enrichment of the "home country" or colonial power. The colonial powers were primarily interested in politically controlling the peoples of their colonies while economically exploiting their resources. Colonies were the economic monopolies of the home country. Thus India, South Africa, Kenya and the other British colonies served as monopolized sources of raw materials for English factories, as well as protected markets for English manufactured goods. Economic development within the English colonies was limited to increasing the production of raw materials needed by English factories and the elimination of goods produced locally, which would compete with goods made in England. Trade between the colonial possessions of the empire and other countries was highly controlled and regulated from London. A similar relationship existed between the home country and the colonies of other colonial powers.

Even if political barriers had not inhibited trade, there were still the problems of geography and distance. International telephone service was extremely limited and most communications had to be sent by mail. International air travel was in its infancy. The vast majority of international travelers went by train or ship. As for moving raw materials and manufactured goods, compared to today, shipping was slow, expensive, and frequently difficult. Thus markets were protected not only by trade barriers, but also geography. As a result, even within the colonial empires, regions were usually self-sufficient in their basic economic needs. The people raised the food they ate, built and furnished the houses they lived in from locally produced goods, and tailored the clothes they wore from locally produced materials. Imports were usually limited to goods or products that could not be made or found locally, while exports usually consisted of goods or products not needed for local use or consumption. The development of the global economy thus required both changes in political structures as well as new technological innovation.

Three major changes have occurred since the end of World War II that have profoundly altered the course of human history and made the developing global economy possible. The most basic of these changes was the disintegration of the colonial empires and the elimination of many of the political barriers to trade. Although the precise number varies depending on how one defines an "independent" or "autonomous" country, at the beginning of World War II there were at best only about sixty politically independent countries in the world. Following the war the colonial empires began to disintegrate. Independence movements had already started in many colonial areas prior to the war, and the war had devastated the economies of many of the colonial powers such as England, France, and the Netherlands. Needing to rebuild their home economies, they lacked the resources to suppress the independence movements in their colonies.

The war also resulted in the United States emerging as the strongest economic and military power in the world. After the war United States began pressuring its European allies to grant independence to their colonies. There were two reasons behind the actions of the United States. First, the United States was ideologically opposed to colonialism, granting independence to the Philippines immediately following the war. Second, U.S. companies wanted direct access to the resources and markets of colonial Africa and Asia. As a result, between 1946 and 1980 eighty-eight new countries were carved out of the old colonial empires and given political independence. The collapse of the Soviet Union and Yugoslavia during the 1990s resulted in the creation of eighteen additional countries. Today there are about 200 independent countries, more than three times the number that existed prior to World War II.

With the end of colonialism, the peoples of Africa and Asia had the freedom to manage their own economic affairs. These "new" countries could now sell their raw materials and products on the global market and purchase imported goods from any country they wished. Even more importantly, these former colonies could now establish local industries to complete with those of the industrialized powers of Western Europe and North America.

The second critical change was in the development of new technologies, associated with production, transportation, and communications. Today we can extract more raw materials and produce more manufactured goods and food using only a fraction of the physical labor required prior to World War II. Technology has greatly improved labor efficiency, allowing people to produce a greater surplus of goods. At the same time the cost of shipping raw materials, food, and manufactured goods, as well as the time in transit, has been dramatically reduced.

Oceangoing cargo ships are still the primary means of international transport. However, ships and shipping have changed dramatically. During World War II the standard military supply ship built by the U.S. government was 440 feet long and capable of carrying 9,000 tons of cargo. In contrast, modern cargo ships are commonly 700 feet long and carry about 25,000 tons of cargo. Even larger are the supertankers, which may be as long as 1,200 feet and capable of carrying 500,000 tons of oil.

The important difference is not just the relative size of the ships but also the speed with which ships can be loaded and unloaded. Fifty years ago cargo was loaded and unloaded piecemeal. Starting in the late 1950s some shippers began loading cargo in 20- and 40-foot boxes, or containers. The containers were loaded at the factory, sent via truck or train to the port, and loaded directly onto the ship by cranes. This greatly increased the speed of loading and unloading. By the late 1960s and early 1970s container shipping became the norm and new cargo ships were being designed and constructed to carry standardized containers. A ship that took ten days to load or unload piecemeal can now be loaded or unloaded in less than a day. Container shipping not only dramatically increased the speed with which goods could be shipped, but drastically reduced labor costs as well. Container ships require smaller crews and many fewer dock workers. The development of container shipping has been one of the key elements in the growth of international trade and thus the global economy.

Just as container shipping has reduced the time and cost of moving goods, airline travel has greatly reduced the time and cost of moving people. Business trips are a critical aspect of international trade. Trips that took days, weeks, and even months in the 1940s and 1950s have been reduced to hours and days. The Concorde—which was recently retired from service—even made it possible for an individual to travel from New York to London and back in a single day.

The last twenty years has been of time of rapid change in information and communications technology. Communications satellites, personal computers, cell phones and other new technologies have revolutionized our communications systems and our abilities to store, access, and analyze information. Today letters, messages, photos, music, videos, and even whole databases can be sent or accessed, while products can be bought or sold and money transferred twenty-four hours a day, instantaneously, to or from any part of the world via the Internet. In terms of communication it does not make any difference if the other company or branch of the company is on the other side of town or the other side of the world. In fact, small companies advertise their merchandise on web pages and sell to customers throughout the world via e-mail. Today one can literally create and operate a global business from a home office. Effective communication is a key element in business, and without the Internet, an integrated global economy could not exist. Technological advancement in transportation and communications has not merely made the world smaller; for many purposes it has made geography irrelevant.

A third factor has been the emergence of international finance. Prior to World War II the international flow of capital was extremely limited. Foreign investment was highly risky, particularly in underdeveloped poorer countries. Whether the loan was to a foreign government or a foreign company, there was always the question of repayment. As long as the empires existed banks and companies would make investments in colonial possessions, knowing that they would have legal protection. However, with the end of colonialism and the emergence of new countries the problem became greater. Most of the peoples in the world today live in underdeveloped countries. The economic growth of these countries requires the development of their infrastructures: communications systems, transportation systems, and even education systems to train workers in skills. The development of infrastructure requires capital, which many of these countries do not have. Similarly, companies in these underdeveloped countries find it difficult to secure sufficient local investment capital for their needs.

In 1945 the World Bank and International Monetary Fund (IMF) were created to help war-ravaged Europe and Japan reestablish their industrial base. These two institutions have played a pivotal role in the creation of the global economy. The World Bank has been the major conduit for economic development loans to underdeveloped nations. The role of the World Bank is now supplemented by numerous European, American, and Japanese banking houses that have become international financiers.

Loans provided to these capital-poor countries have allowed them to more quickly adopt high-cost technology and increase their economic productivity. With these funds, underdeveloped countries have constructed irrigation systems, expanded transportation and communication systems, expanded port facilities, and developed local industries. In the past decade alone these loans have amounted to hundreds of billions of dollars. An unappreciated consequence of these loans is the stimulation of exports of developed countries, because most of these funds are used to purchase needed technology and equipment from the United States, Europe, and Japan. At the same time most of the economic development projects funded by these loan have focused on increasing the production of goods and raw materials needed by these industrialized countries, which in turn lowers the global market prices of these items.

In the global economy money flows both ways across international boundaries in search of greater profits. U.S. banks, companies, and individuals have more than $4 trillion invested in other countries. Conversely, foreign banks, companies, and individuals have similar amounts invested in the United States. Of the $3.5 trillion in U.S. government debt, 38 percent is owed to foreign individuals or banks, with the largest share owned by Japanese. Japanese banks in turn have made more than $290 billion in loans to other Asian countries.

Globalization: The Continuing Process

While the global economy is already dramatically affecting the lives of all virtually everyone, it is still in the process of developing. Some issues remain to be resolved and some new economic institutions are starting to evolve. The process of globalizating the world market is far from complete.

Although we have a global economy, we still lack free trade. Every one of the 200 or so countries in the world still has regulations concerning imports and exports, as well as it own labor laws, environmental laws, and other business regulations. In addition, almost every country still has its own currency, currency regulations, and laws concerning banking and other financial concerns. Regulation of the economy is one of the primary concerns of government. However, in a fully integrated and operative global economy there can be no local or national differences. The World Trade Organization is in the process of attempting to negotiate the elimination of all import and export laws or controls as well as any other laws that inhibit the free flow of goods or services between countries. The result will be free trade, a world in which companies and individuals may buy and sell any legal goods or services, at any price agreed upon, in any country in the world, without government regulation. In all disputes, the World Trade Organization, not the governments involved, would be the final judge.

The global economy also requires international control of currencies, banking, and other financial transactions. The International Monetary Fund is assuming the role as regulator of international monetary transactions. Most countries have their own currencies. Exchange rates for currencies are complex and volatile. In international financial transfers, varying exchange rates are an added expense. Recognizing that the use of different currencies makes integrating economies more difficult, most of the countries of the European Union changed to a single currency, the Euro, in January 2002. Some have suggested that a fully integrated global economy will require a single global monetary unit and the elimination of all national currencies.

Traditional we have thought of corporations, like individuals, as having national identities. Ford, General Motors, and General Electric are "American" companies. These companies are incorporated in the United States, their stock is traded on the New York Stock Exchange, and their corporate headquarters are in the United States. However, companies such as these are increasingly becoming international, manufacturing and selling products throughout the world. Globalization is eroding the link between corporations and their countries of origin. This results in the emergence of what are now being termed transnational corporations. For centuries, if not longer, some companies have produced goods for export and had overseas offices and operations. Thus the distinction between traditional national corporations and transnational corporations is not precise. A *transnational corporation* is one that has most of its employees, produces and sells most of its products or services, and generates most of its gross revenues outside the national boundaries of its "home" country.

Nokia, a Finnish company known primarily for its cellular phones, is an example of a transnational corporation. Just prior to the collapse of tech stocks in 2000, Nokia had the highest capitalization value (the total value of it stock) of any company in Europe.

Originally a paper manufacturer, Nokia was founded in 1865. In 1967 Nokia merged with the Finish Rubber Works and Finish Cable Works, the latter producing telephone wire and cable. The new Nokia quickly focused on telecommunications, producing first radio telephones and later data modems. By the 1980s Nokia was becoming a major producer of computers, monitors, and TV sets. In 1987 Nokia produced the original handheld portable telephone. The 1990s was a period of rapid growth for the company as it maintained its position as the major producer of cellular phones in the world. Today Nokia markets products in more than 130 countries, has research and development projects and programs in 15 different countries (including the United States, Canada, Australia, Singapore, Japan, South Korea, Spain, Germany, and England), and produces components and assembled products in 10 different countries (United States, Mexico, Brazil, Malaysia, China, South Korea, Japan Hungary, Germany, and England).

The production of components and assembled products shows the problem of determining national origin of goods in the global economy. Nokia has six major suppliers: Phillips Electronics, a Dutch company, produces their speakers in Austria and display screens in China; Sanyo Electric, a Japanese company, produces their barrier (a component of a phone) in Mexico; Hitachi makes its power amplification modules in Japan; Infineon Technologies make its semiconductor chips in Germany; and R.F. Micro Devices and Texas Instruments produce their radio frequency integrated circuits and digital signal processors in the United States. Today most Nokia products are designed by non-Finish engineers and technicians, manufactured and assembled in countries other than Finland, and sold in 130 countries in the world, in order to produce wealth and profits shared by investors from all parts of the world. Its corporate headquarters may still be located in Finland and its major management decisions are still made in Finland, but is Nokia still a Finnish company, or is it a global company with its main offices in Helsinki?

As the global economy continues to evolve all major corporations, in order to economically compete, will have to become transnational corporations. The result will be a change in the relationship between a country and "its" corporations. It used to be said that "what is good for General Motors is good for America." There was truth in this saying in that the economic health of one could not be separated from that of the other. With transnational corporations the same cannot be said. What is economically good for a transnational corporation may adversely affect the economy of its "home" country. We are already experiencing some of this as American companies close their domestic plants and shift their production to Mexico, China, or some other country with low labor costs.

Population Growth and Inequities in the Global Economy

Probably the least controversial aspect of globalization has been the improvement in health of the world's peoples. At the end of World War II the World Health Organization (WHO) was created as part of the United Nations to address global health concerns. Working with private and government health organizations and agencies, the WHO defined issues and attempted to direct resources to particular health problems. Of particular concern were infant mortality rates in most of the underdeveloped countries of the world. By improving sanitation systems, nutritional standards, and health care delivery systems in underdeveloped countries, WHO has helped to drastically lower infant mortality rates.

In addition, WHO has developed programs for the eradication of epidemic diseases. In 1946 malaria was a major health concern throughout most of the Americas, Africa, Asia, and the Pacific. In India alone it was estimated that 800,000 people a year died from the disease, while globally several million people died annually. Malaria is an insect-borne disease spread from one infected human to another by anopheles mosquitoes. Lacking vaccines, the only way to eliminate the disease was to destroy the mosquito populations that spread it. Using DDT, in 1948 WHO launched a program for the elimination of malaria. By the 1960s widespread use of DDT had dramatically reduced the death rate from malaria. In the mid-1960s, India reported no deaths from the disease. At one point it was thought that malaria might be eliminated altogether. However, the discovery that DDT had numerous environmentally destructive side effects led to limitations on its use as a pesticide. This, together with the evolution of a new DDT-resistant anopheles mosquito, ended the hope of eliminating malaria. Even though the malaria program was not totally successful, tens of millions of lives were saved.

Smallpox has been a major health problem since the ancient period. This virus, spread by human hosts, either through the air or by touch, can kill up to 40 percent of an infected population. In the 1960s there were on average between 10 and 15 million cases a year, and 2 million deaths from smallpox. In 1967 WHO launched a vaccination campaign designed to eliminate smallpox and within ten years totally eliminated the virus. In 1980, after three years during which no new cases were reported from anywhere in the world, WHO was able to announce that the smallpox virus had been eliminated.

In addition to the malaria and smallpox programs, WHO continues to work to improve health conditions by assisting in the development of health care delivery systems throughout the world. As a result infant mortality have declined dramatically and life expectances have increased in virtually every part of the global. In the past fifty years the worlds population has jumped from 2.5 billion to more than 6 billion people. WHO's efforts have been the primary factor in this rapid growth.

Although health conditions among all peoples have improved, birth rates differ widely. As a result some regions of the world have seen their populations grow rapidly. The most striking differences are between the developed and undeveloped world. The birth rates of the developed countries of Western Europe, North America, and Japan have dropped dramatically. In the most extreme cases some of these countries now have negative growth rates. In Italy, for example, if the present trend continues, the population will decline from its present 57 million (2000), to 45 million by 2050. Japan also has a negative growth rate which, if it continues at it present rate, will result in its population declining from 126 million to 101 million by 2050.

In sharp contrast are the birth rates of the people of sub-Saharan Africa, Latin America, and most of Asia. The populations of these regions are increasing at a rate averaging almost 2 percent per year or more. In the next half century it is projected that the population of India will increase by more than 500 million, while that of neighboring Pakistan will jump by almost 200 million. In 1950, Nigeria, the largest country of sub-Saharan Africa, had a population of only 31 million; by 2000 that population had grown to 123 million. Even given a projected decline in birth rate, it is still estimated that by the year 2050, Nigeria will be home to more than 300 million people.

The regional differences in population growth rates are rapidly changing the geographical distribution of the world population. If we compare population changes by regions and by percentages, and limit it to only to the period from 1950 to 2025, we can see quickly how significant the change will be (see Table 3 below).

Table 3

	1950 (%)	2025 (%)
Developed Countries	33.1	15.9
Undeveloped Countries	66.9	84.1

(Source: Adapted from Robbins: 148.)

By 2025, the population of the developed countries of the world will constitute only about one-sixth of the world's population. The rapidly growing majority of the world population is both impoverished and non-Western in cultural heritage.

There is no doubt that the emergence of the global economy has greatly benefited the developed world and the United States in particular. In terms of tangible material wealth alone Americans can see a vast change in their lifestyle. In the past 50 years the size of the average new American home has more than doubled, from 900 square feet to more than 2,000 square feet. The quantity of our material positions has grown proportionally to fill the new space. Fifty years ago the typical American family owned only a single automobile; today that same family owns two or more. Today we also eat out more and travel more and farther. The developed countries of Western Europe and Japan have seen similar increases in relative wealth. In contrast, most of the underdeveloped countries of Latin America, Africa, and Asia have not participated in this new prosperity. The result has been increasing inequalities in the distribution of wealth in world. In 1960 it was estimated that the richest 20 percent of the world's population had 30 times more income than the poorest 20 percent. By 1999 this ratio had risen to 74 to 1 and was still increasing. It is not just that many people in the world are not sharing in this new wealth; their standards of living are actually declining. Since 1980 per capita incomes in more than a third of the countries of the world have declined. Today 1.2 billion people, one-fifth of the world's population, are attempting to exist on incomes of less than $1 per day. The distribution of the world's wealth has become so skewed that the total assets of the three richest individuals in the world exceed the annual income of the poorest 600 million, while the richest 200 individuals in the world have wealth that exceeds the annual income of the poorest 2.4 billion people.

The problem is not just that a significant wealth gap exists between the rich and poor of the world, but that the gap is rapidly increasing and there appears to be no way to reverse the trend. It is not merely a question of half or more of the world's population left behind by the global economy; they are being left out of participation. In the new global economy these people do not play a significant role either as producers or consumers. A people's ability to participate in, let alone prosper from, the evolving global economy is directly linked to their access to information and communications technology. In most countries in the world only a small minority of the population has access to telephones, let alone state-of-the-art information and communications technology. What some have termed a digital divide now separates the world's peoples into those who have access to this new technology and those whose access is limited or nonexistent.

The new technology is expensive and the countries that lack it are poor. Presently forty-one countries in Africa, Asia, and Latin America are termed "heavily indebted nations," meaning that they cannot even make the interest payments on their existing foreign loans. They are not just poor and indebted, their debts are increasing. Since 1980 the combined debts of these countries have risen $55 billion to more than $200 billion. Not only do the people of these countries lack this new technology, they lack the capital to acquire it and the educational skills to make use of it if they had it. They are caught in a cycle of increasing poverty from which there appears no escape.

If we look at the world as a whole, we find that both the global economy and human populations are growing rapidly. However, if we begin to examine this issue country by country or region by region, we quickly discover that there is an inverse correlation between economic growth and population growth. Generally speaking, countries and regions with high economic growth usually have low population growth rates, while countries with rapid population growth most commonly have slow or even negative economic growth rates.

Sub-Saharan Africa in many ways typifies the problems of the underdeveloped regions of the world. The people of this region are basically dependent upon agriculture. Relative to their population, they have limited marketable natural resources and little industry. Not only do these countries have poorly developed educational and transportation systems and a lack of information and communications technology, they do not have the financial resources available to acquire or develop them. With the highest birth rate in the world, sub-Saharan Africa has already reached the crisis point. For the past two decades the populations of these countries have grown much faster than their economies. Increasing populations have resulted in an overuse of agricultural resources and a deterioration of the land base. Since the early 1960s per capita food production has dropped by 16 percent. As a result, today the people of this region are over 20 percent poorer in economic terms than they were in the mid-1970s.

With more than 500 million people sub-Saharan Africa is already overpopulated. It is estimated that about 40 percent of the region's population live on less than $1 per day and are chronically undernourished. In the next fifty years it is estimated that this population will grow by an additional one billion people. The countries of sub-Saharan Africa face the virtually impossible task of developing their economies to meet the needs of this expanding population. Economic conditions are only going to become worse as an ever- increasing percentage of the population goes hungry. Similar, although not as severe, conditions exist in much of Latin America and Asia. Economic development cannot keep pace with population growth and already impoverished people are becoming poorer and poorer.

There are two possible solutions to the growing economic problems of the underdeveloped world. One answer would be to create massive economic development programs to increase agricultural and industrial production, linked to programs to reduce the population growth rates. However, such programs would literally cost trillions of dollars and would have to be financed by the developed countries of the world. The only other solution is for a mass migration of people from the underdeveloped to the developed countries of world. This migration has already started.

The greatest movement of people in human history is already under way. This migration is taking two forms. First is rural to urban migration, which is occurring in every country in the world. Second is the migration of people from poorer countries to wealthier countries. Just before World War II, about 50 percent of the total population of the United States and Europe was urban, compared with only about 8 to 10 percent for Africa and Asia and 25 percent for Latin America. Today, about 75 percent of Americans and 70 percent of Europeans are city dwellers. However, the urban populations of Asia and Africa have jumped to between 25 and 30 percent, and in Latin America the urban population has increased to more than 60 percent. The growth rate of urbanization has thus been highest outside Europe and North America. In fact, the world's most rapidly growing cities are located in underdeveloped nations: Bandung (Indonesia), Lagos (Nigeria), Karachi (Pakistan), Baghdad (Iraq), and Bogotá (Colombia). In some of these cities the growth rate has been phenomenal. In the 1950s, Bogotá had a population of only about 650,000; by 1995 its population was more than 5 million. Similar increases are common in many Latin American, Asian, and African nations. Most cities in the underdeveloped world lack the large industrial complexes capable of employing the great masses of people migrating into them, but their small-scale industries, transportation services, and government jobs, although limited, offer greater economic opportunities than do the increasingly overcrowded rural regions.

Whereas most migration has been within countries, the growing trend is toward international migration. The United Nations estimates that 150 million people, or almost 3 percent of the world's population, now live in a country other that the one in which they were born. Many argue that this number is a conservative figure. The main difficulty in discussing internation migration is that it takes so many forms. There are legal immigrants who are in the process of becoming citizens of another country; however, not all countries allow such immigrants. There are other immigrants who have temporary legal status to live in another country: guest workers, students, and *refugees*. Then there are illegal immigrants, individuals who have illegally taken up residence in another country. The distinction between these categories is often blurred. In many cases individuals who come as "students" and "refugees" are in reality coming in search of jobs.

As their industrial economies expanded during the 1950s and 1960s, many Western European countries began experiencing labor shortages. West Germany initiated a "guest-worker" program to actively recruit foreign laborers, first in southern Europe, Italy, and Spain, and later in Yugoslavia and Turkey. Concurrently, French factories began recruiting Arab workers from their then North African colonies, particularly Algeria. In the 1950s, England began experiencing an influx of West Indians from its possessions in the Caribbean. In the 1960s, a wave of Pakistani and Indian immigrants also settled in England. Other Western European countries experienced a similar phenomenon, although usually on a smaller scale.

By the early 1970s, when the economic growth of Western Europe began to slow, large non-European communities were well established in most of the major cities. When West Germany ended its guest-worker program in 1974, it had hosted 2.5 million foreign workers, a number equal to more than 10 percent of its total labor force. Through various means the West German government tried to repatriate these guest workers and their families, but failed. France, England, and other Western European countries have considered stricter immigration laws to stop the continuing influx of African and Asian workers, but the number of new immigrants is increasing despite tighter controls. By the 1990 almost 10 percent of the population of Western Europe were recent immigrants.

The United States has always allowed for relatively large numbers of legal immigrants. Since World War II, about 25 percent of American population growth has been the result of immigration. However, migration patterns to the United States have changed dramatically in the post-war period. In the 1950s, well over one-half the immigrants to the United States were still coming from Europe; the second largest group, about one-third, were coming from Latin America. In the 1960s, the flood of immigrants began to increase. From only about 300,000 persons per year in the 1960s, the number of immigrants jumped to more than 400,000 per year in the 1970s and to more than 700,000 per year in the 1980s. As the number of immigrants increased, their origins shifted markedly. Proportionally, the number of Latin American immigrants remained about the same, while European immigration declined. The major change was in the number of Asian arrivals, from less than 10 percent of all immigrants in 1950 to more than 30 percent by the 1990s. As a result, between 1980 and 2000 the number of Asian-Americans almost tripled, from 3.5 million (1.5 percent) to more than 10.2 million (3.6 percent), whereas the number of Latin Americans more than doubled, from 14.5 million (6.4 percent) to more than 35 million (12.5 percent).

Although Europe and North America have been the primary destinations for most international migrants, other regions with high income, labor shortages, or both have experienced major influxes of immigrants. Many of the oil-rich Arab countries—Libya, Saudi Arabia, Kuwait, Quatar, Oman, and the United Arab Emirates—have recruited foreign workers from India, Pakistan, Bangladesh, and Egypt, and from among Palestinian refugees. Indeed, in some of the smaller of these countries foreign workers outnumber native Arabs. For example, foreign workers constitute almost 60 percent of the population of Kuwait.

Over the last twenty years international immigration patterns have changed. While the main objective of most immigrants is still to reach either the United States or Western Europe, any wealthier country can be the destination. Whereas in the past most immigrants to the developed countries were from Latin America, East Asia, or South Asia, the numbers of immigrants from Africa, the Middle East, and the former republics of the Soviet Union are growing. Although in recent decades the United States and the countries of Western Europe have increased their legal immigration quotas in all categories, the numbers of individuals wanting to immigrate have increased far more rapidly. The reasons why the ranks of immigrants are growing so dramatically are simple. Every part of the world, thanks in large part to satellite dishes, has television; most of the programs are American or Western European. On television people see life in the developed countries and realize that there is an alternative to the desperate poverty around them, if only they can get there.

The borders of the developed countries of the world are being overwhelmed by increasing waves of illegal immigrants who will take any risks to escape from their world of hopeless poverty. Illegals from Mexico cross the deserts of the southwest on foot with no water. Migrants from Nigeria, Ghana, and other West African countries travel cross the Sahara on foot, on camels, and in old trucks to try and reach the Mediterranean coast where, if they are lucky, they might find a small boat that will take them to Spain and Europe. Some individuals have literally walked most of the way from Afghanistan to Germany. Chinese families mortgage everything they own to pay a smuggler to take one of their family members to the United States or Europe. Individuals with no property place themselves in debt bondage to criminal gangs of smugglers, working their debt off in illegal sweatshops or brothels in New York City, Rome, or some other city in the developed world. For many of these people, no personal expense is too great or no danger too frightening to stop them from attempting to reach their objective.

Most of the estimated 9 million illegal immigrants in the United States are from Latin America; however, they come from all parts of the world. The actual number is unknown. The only reliable figure we have is that 1.6 million illegals were deported in 2000.

The problem with illegals in Western Europe is not as great as in the United States, but it is rapidly growing. It is estimated that there are already between 3 and 3.5 million illegal immigrants. This number is growing by an additional 500,000 a year. The potential problem for Western Europe is best shown by the growing immigrant population of the bordering country of Yugoslavia. In 1997 Yugoslavia began admitting Chinese on student visas. In spite of its poor economy, economic sanctions, and bombing by NATO, in four years the Chinese "student" community in Belgrade has grown to number between 75,000 and 100,000.

Other developed countries are also facing the problem of growing populations of illegal workers. Japan estimates that about 250,000 Koreans, Filipinos, Chinese, and Thais are illegally living and working in Japan. Korea estimates its number of illegals at about 200,000, and Australia estimates that it has an illegal population of about 60,000. However, the country with proportionally the greatest problem is South Africa, which in spite of a high unemployment rate, has an estimated 4 million illegals out of a total population of 43 million. The economy of South Africa may not be good by American or Western European standards, but compared to those of the war-torn countries of central Africa, it is a paradise.

Already many people in the United States and Western Europe are complaining of the growing numbers of immigrants. The same is true in other countries that feel themselves inundated by foreigners. In Libya there have been riots in which immigrants have been killed, and in South Africa some of the illegals have been murdered. If people think the problem is bad today, they need only wait for tomorrow. If the economic inequalities of the global economy are not corrected, and the economies of the underdeveloped countries are not dramatically improved, the rate of immigration will only increase. There are hundreds of millions more only waiting for the opportunity to move.

Consequences of Globalization and the Global Economy

Globalization is multifaceted and its effects and consequences are far reaching. The global economy is creating an increasing economic interdependence of the world's people, not just in technology, manufactured goods, and clothing, but food as well. The global economy is producing tremendous new wealth, while at the same time producing poverty and an increasingly skewed distribution in wealth. The global economy is resulting in the greatest migration in human history, which is changing the ethnic mix of all the world's cities, especially the cities of Western Europe and the United States. In Western Europe today one sees increasing numbers of people from Africa, the Middle East, and all parts of Asia. In the United States one sees not only increasing numbers of peoples from Africa, the Middle East and Asia, but Latin America as well. The global media is a marketing tool that is attempting to sell to the world not only material goods, but Western (primarily American) lifestyles, values, and beliefs. Some argue that, whether intended or not, the global media now serves as a means of Western cultural propaganda that is threatening and eroding the cultural traditions of the non-Western peoples of the world.

The events of September 11, 2001, when nineteen men hijacked jetliners and crashed into the World Trade Center, the Pentagon, and a field in rural Pennsylvania, have left a deep impression not just in the minds of Americans, but people throughout most of the world. Why would people hate the United States so much that they would sacrifice their own lives in order to inflect such damage and carnage? It is obvious that they were part of a much larger, well-organized, and well-financed Middle Eastern Islamic group. As many commentators have pointed out, the attack does not appear to have been directly related to American support for Israel against the Palestinians, or any other particular action of the United States. The issues are much deeper and more fundamental.

In his recent book, *Runaway World*, Anthony Giddens (2000, 22) states, "The battleground of the twenty-first century will pit fundamentalism against cosmopolitan tolerance." By fundamentalists Giddens means those who are adherents of traditional (non-Western) cultural values and practices. In contrast, cosmopolitan people are those who have embraced the cultural values and practices of globalization, in other words, people who have or have adopted Western cultural traditions. Thus conflict in the twenty-first century will be between the West and the traditional rest. Giddens is not the first to suggest that there will be increasing conflicts between peoples from different cultural traditions or "civilizations." Samuel Huntington (1996), in his study, *The Clash of Civilizations,* suggested the increasing possibility of such conflicts. The difference is that Giddens clearly places these conflicts within the context of globalization.

Over the past forty years oil production has resulted in prosperity for many of the peoples of the Middle East. As a result of this wealth, few non-Western peoples have been as exposed to Western cultural influences as the Islamic peoples of this region. Tens of thousands of Middle Eastern students have studied at universities, colleges, and technical schools in the United States and Europe. Still more individuals have visited the United States and Europe on business or vacation trips. Even those who have remained at home have not escaped exposure to Western culture. In most of the countries of the modern Middle East Western cultural influences are pervasive: television programs, movies, music, clothing styles, and Web sites. Even Western foods are locally available: McDonald's is now found in many of the major cities. But many clerics and traditional leaders in the Islamic Middle East have come to view Western culture as the ultimate source of evil and degeneracy, corrupting their people and threatening to destroy their traditional values, norms, and beliefs. In 1979, the government of Iran was overthrown, and an Islamic republic established, which has worked to eliminate Western influences from Iranian society. Anwar Sadat, the President of Egypt was assassinated in 1981 by religious extremists, but they were unable to gain control of the Egyptian government. More recently the Taliban gained control of Afghanistan and established an Islamic republic, attempting to remove all foreign influences. For the past few years the Western-oriented government of Algeria has been locked in an increasingly vicious and bloody civil war with Islamic fundamentalists.

Throughout the Islamic Middle East there are growing fundamentalist movements whose objectives are to overthrow existing secular governments and reestablish Islamic cultural supremacy by erasing Western cultural influence. To these people the Western-controlled global economy and the growing influence of Western culture are inseparable. They see the United States as the center of the Western world and thus the ultimate source of their problems.

Globalization has made the world smaller and geography no longer relevant. The oceans of the world no longer separate us or protect us. The problems of one region of the world quickly become the problems of another, and the problems of the Middle East have become the problems of America.

Part IV: Domestic Tensions

Due to the intense media scrutiny of the terrorist attacks and the fact that the terrorists of September 11, 2001 were of Middle Eastern origin, there is the potential for prejudice and discrimination against Americans that follow the Islamic religion and toward individuals of Middle Eastern ethnicity. Since September 11, an escalating number of hate crimes have been reported against Americans of Middle Eastern descent. In order to address this phenomenon, a series of essays has been included in this section that aims to provoke further thought on the pressing issues of racial and ethnic prejudice in the United States. Authors Margaret Andersen and Howard Taylor examine prejudice from a sociological perspective in their textbook, Sociology: Understanding a Diverse Society, Second Edition *(2002). Following this is an essay from Jonathan R. White on the defensive role of law enforcement subsequent to September 11th. This material was obtained from his book* Defending the Homeland: Domestic Intelligence, Law Enforcement, and Security *(Wadsworth, 2003). At the end of this section, you will find a self-quiz, which will help you explore various commonly held prejudices. The quiz was obtained from Diana Kendall's text,* Sociology In Our Times: The Essentials, Third Edition *(2002).*

A. Prejudice
This excerpt was written by Margaret L. Andersen and Howard F. Taylor, Sociology: Understanding a Diverse Society, Second Edition (Wadsworth, 2002).

Prejudice is the evaluation of a social group, and individuals within that group, based on conceptions about the social group that are held despite facts that contradict it and that involve both prejudgment and misjudgment (Allport, 1954; Pettigrew, 1971; Jones, 1997). Prejudices are usually defined as negative predispositions or evaluations, rarely positive. Thinking ill of people only because they are members of group X is prejudice. The negative evaluation arises solely because the person is seen as a member of group X, without regard to countervailing traits or characteristics the person may have. A negative prejudice against someone not in one's own social group is often accompanied by a positive prejudice in favor of someone who is in one's own group. Thus, the prejudiced person will have negative attitudes about a member of an *out-group* (any group other than one's own) and positive attitudes about someone simply because he or she is in one's *in-group* (any group one considers one's own).

Most people disavow racial or ethnic prejudice, yet the vast majority of us carry around some prejudices, whether about racial–ethnic groups, men and women, old and young, upper class and lower class, or straight and gay. Prejudice is what social scientists call a variable—it varies from person to person. Five decades of research have shown definitively that people who are more prejudiced are also more likely to stereotype others by race or ethnicity, and often by gender, than those who are less prejudiced (Adorno et al., 1950; Jones, 1997; Taylor et al., 1997; Worchel et al., 2000). Nevertheless, everyone possesses some prejudices.

Prejudice based on race or ethnicity is called *racial-ethnic prejudice*. In-groups and out-groups in this case are defined along racial or ethnic lines. If you are a Latino and dislike an Anglo only because he or she is White, then this constitutes prejudice. It is a negative judgment ("prejudgment") based on race and ethnicity and very little else. In this example, Latino is the in-group and White is the out-group. If the Latino individual attempts to justify these feelings by arguing that "all Whites have the same bad character," then the Latino is using a stereotype as justification for the prejudice. Similarly, *gender prejudice* exists in our society. There are negative prejudices based on gender, and in-group and out-group are defined by gender. Finally, there is *class prejudice*, the negative evaluation of people solely on the basis of their social class, but little reference to anything else about them. Note that prejudice can be held by any group against another. Thus, African Americans can be prejudiced against Whites or against Hispanics and Asian Americans. African Americans of West Indian (Caribbean) descent may be prejudiced against non-West Indian African Americans. Such prejudice does exist, although sociological research has found that recent concerns that there is a backlash of prejudice by African Americans against Hispanics and Asian Americans is generally less than prejudice by White Americans toward these groups (Cummings and Lambert, 1997).

Prejudice is also revealed in the phenomenon of ethnocentrism. *Ethnocentrism* is the belief that one's group is superior to all other groups. The ethnocentric person feels that his or her own group is moral, just, and right and that an out-group —and thus any member of the out-group—is immoral, unjust, wrong, distrustful, or criminal. The ethnocentric individual uses his or her own in-group as the standard against which all other groups are compared. Generally, the greater the difference between groups, the more harshly the out-group will be judged by an ethnocentric individual and the more prejudiced that person will be against members of the out-group.

The Effects of Prejudice

Our judgments about other people can hardly escape being influenced by our feelings (prejudices) about their group as a whole. Several studies show this dramatically (Sweeney and Haney, 1992; Ugwuegbu, 1979). In one study, White students were asked to serve as jurors in a mock rape trial. Each read a hypothetical, but very realistic, account of the rape of a nineteen-year-old White woman by a twenty-one-year-old man. Four different accounts (experimental conditions) were used. In one account, the alleged rapist was a Black man, and the evidence against him was strong (both the female victim and an eyewitness identified the rapist). In another, the alleged rapist was Black and the evidence against him was weak (neither the female victim nor the eyewitness could identify the rapist). In two other accounts, the evidence followed a similar pattern, but the rapist was a White man. The results were interesting. On a scale of blame, the Black man was always blamed more than the White man, *regardless* of whether the evidence was weak or strong. The strength of the evidence made a slight difference. Both alleged rapists were perceived as more culpable when the evidence was strong as opposed to weak. The point is that race has an effect on the amount of blame attributed to the alleged rapist—*in addition* to the effect of the strength of the evidence. Race by itself has a clear and separate—even bigger—effect.

The results were similar no matter what the race of the juror, although a Black juror was somewhat less likely than a White juror to attribute blame to the Black alleged rapist. Strikingly similar results have been obtained, when possible, in actual rape trials in real courts by comparing trials with defendants of a different race and trials with differing evidence strength (Loewen, 1982; Sweeney and Haney, 1992).

Racial and ethnic prejudice also has a marked effect on people's political views and on how they vote. This is shown in studies that incorporate a separate measure of the amount of the individual's prejudice and relate this to voting preferences. For example, when Jesse Jackson, the Black minister and political activist, ran for the Democratic presidential nomination in 1984, he was opposed most by Whites who were highly prejudiced, whereas less prejudiced Whites were more likely to favor him (Sears et al., 1988). The difference was attributable to prejudice itself, not the objective advantages and disadvantages of the candidate.

Whether one is for or against affirmative action and similar programs, one's prejudice predicts fairly accurately how one will respond to a particular program, regardless of relevant, objective facts about the situation. For example, the more prejudiced a White person is, the more likely he or she will oppose busing to achieve racial balance in schools (Jessor, 1988; Kluegel and Bobo, 1993). Prejudice is not the only reason one might oppose busing, but prejudice is part of the picture.

The same holds true with regard to affirmative action policies on behalf of Asian Americans. The more strongly an individual is prejudiced against Asian Americans, the more that person will object to any governmental program that benefits Asian Americans, such as monetary reparations to the Japanese American families who were unjustly interned in concentration camps after U.S. entry into World War II. The same is true for other kinds of educational and political programs geared to benefit Asian Americans (Takaki, 1989; Takagi, 1992).

Prejudice and Socialization

Where does racial-ethnic prejudice come from? How do moderately or highly prejudiced people end up that way? People are not born with stereotypes and prejudices. Research shows that they are learned and internalized through the socialization process, including both *primary socialization* (family, peers, and teachers) and *secondary socialization* (such as the media). Children imitate the attitudes of their parents, peers, and teachers. If the parent complains about "Japs taking away jobs" from Americans, then the child grows up thinking negatively about the Japanese, including Japanese Americans. Attitudes about race are formed early in childhood, at about age three or four (Allport, 1954; Van Ausdale and Feagin, 1996). There is a very close correlation between the racial and ethnic attitudes of parents and those of their children (Ashmore and DelBoca, 1976). The more ethnically or racially prejudiced the parent, the more ethnically or racially prejudiced on average will be the child. Later in life, peers will reinforce these negative feelings, for example, by jeering at Japanese American children on their way to school in the morning.

A major vehicle for the communication of racial-ethnic attitudes to both young and old is the media, especially television, magazines, newspapers, and books. For many decades, African Americans, Hispanics, Native Americans, and Asians were rarely presented in the media, and then only in negatively stereotyped roles. The Chinese were shown in movies, magazines, and early television in the 1950s as bucktoothed buffoons who ran shirt laundries. Japanese Americans were depicted as sneaky and Untrustworthy. Hispanics were shown as either ruthless banditos or playful, happy-go-lucky "Pedros" who took long siestas. American Indians were presented as either villains or subservient characters such as the Lone Ranger's famed sidekick, Tonto. Finally, there is the drearily familiar image of the Black person as subservient, lazy, clowning, and bug-eyed, a stereotypical image that persisted from the late nineteenth century all the way through the 1950s and early 1960s (Thibodeau, 1989).

The late 1960s, which included the Black Power movement and greatly increased civil rights activity in the country, saw some improvements in media stereotypes, which continued into the 1970s and 1980s. During this time, the media became somewhat less culpable in fostering racial and ethnic prejudice. TV programs such as The Cosby Show, featuring an African American doctor (played by Bill Cosby), his lawyer wife (played by Phylicia Rashaad), their well-educated children, and their positive interactions with Whites and Asians, may have contributed to blunting anti-Black prejudice. The Huxtables were a well-to-do family headed by Black professionals and thus could serve as positive role models for Black youth, but they also underscore what African Americans and other minorities in society have not attained. As one critic wryly noted from observing other Black sitcoms, Black people seem to be doing better on TV than in real life (Gates, 1992).

Despite the Huxtables, careful content analyses have shown that improvements in the portrayal of minorities on television have been minimal. For example, positive crossrace interactions have always been infrequent, even into the 1990s. During this period, positive interactions between Blacks and Whites (those in which Blacks and Whites interact as professional equals or friends) have been a mere five percent or less of total interactions, including dramas, comedies, and other types of television shows (Wei et al., 1990).

Arab Americans: Confronting Prejudice

WHENEVER violent confrontations in the Middle East reach one of their periodic surges, Marvin Wingfield braces for the worst: ethnic taunts, stereotypes in the mass media, and violence against Arab Americans.

"The pattern seems to be that whenever there is a crisis in the Mideast, the incidence of hate crimes against Arab Americans increases," says Wingfield, coordinator of conflict resolution for the American-Arab Anti-Discrimination Committee (ADC) in Washington, D.C. "It becomes even more pronounced when the United States is involved directly."

The backlash, Wingfield notes, is simply one manifestation of centuries-old misperceptions in the West about the nature of Arab culture. Colonial arrogance, he says, fostered stereotypes of Arabs as camel-riding hedonists and devious traders. The more modern stereotype of the "Muslim terrorist" led initially to false assumptions about the Oklahoma City bombing.

Another offshoot of this arrogance, Wingfield points out, is the tendency of many white Americans to view other broad segments of the population as homogeneous. References to "the black community," for example, ignore the diversity among African Americans and their interests. Similarly, "the Arab World" is vast and varied. Most Arabs speak Arabic, and most are Islamic, but neither attribute is a prerequisite for "Arab-ness."

Part of the ADC's mission is to help combat stereotypes and reduce anti-Arab hate crimes through educational and political programs. A large part of this effort involves encouraging Arab Americans to play higher profile roles in their communities.

The ADC has prepared guidelines for community activists to follow in trying to increase the presence and awareness of Arab culture in school districts. Called "Working With School Systems," it describes various scenarios for involvement, ranging from volunteering at the classroom level to lobbying for district-wide curriculum development. One notable success occurred in Portland, Oregon, where Arab American activists persuaded the local newspaper, The Oregonian, to include a special Mideast page in its annual "Newspapers in Education" issue.

In metro Detroit, several programs through public schools and nonprofit organizations work to bridge differences between Arab Americans and the broader community. An organization called Arab-Jewish Friends runs an annual contest in which Arab and Jewish high school students cowrite essays. It helps the students break down their own stereotypes by working with students from cultures with whom they have historically been at odds.

"We have them write about issues that are important to Arabs and Jews," says Jeannie Weiner, one of the contest's founders. "It's good for them to put these thoughts down in writing. And it's good for us because we can use the essays as tools to show what the kids are thinking."

Another project, directed by Wayne State University's Center for Peace and Conflict Studies, brought together students from high schools in suburban Dearborn, where metro Detroit's Arab-Muslim population is concentrated, to negotiate a contract for behavior among Arab and non-Arab students. They quickly found common ground in their dissatisfaction with the district's multicultural programs and petitioned school officials for classes in such topics as world religions.

Little came of the demands, but the students learned that they have more in common than they thought, says Mickey Petera, assistant director of the Peace and Conflict Studies Department. "We need to start at the elementary and preschool levels," she says, "and raise a generation of students that can get along."

SOURCE: Teaching Tolerance (Spring 1997): 49. This article is reprinted by permission of Teaching Tolerance, a publication of the Southern Poverty Law Center.

B. The Defensive Role of Law Enforcement
This essay was obtained from Jonathan R. White, Defending the Homeland: Domestic Intelligence, Law Enforcement, and Security *(Wadsworth, 2003).*

Gathering and analyzing information are the most effective tools in counterterrorism's offensive arsenal. Yet, intelligence and aggressive police action will inevitably fail, and terrorists will eventually thwart the most aggressive law enforcement measures. In truth, the best offense will falter at times. Therefore, state and local law enforcement agencies need to prepare defensive plans; that is, they need to be prepared to react to terrorism. While a strategy based solely on defensive concepts leaves all the initiative with terrorist groups, ignoring the need to protect the public with defensive measures is irresponsible. In addition, even defensive actions can be offensive. For example, enhanced security may uncover a plan to attack a facility, or visible patrol presence may deter an attack. It is important to understand the symbolic nature of terrorist attacks and to balance security needs with basic freedoms. State and local agencies should plan operations within the context of multijurisdictional responses and prepare a response for weapons of mass destruction. Understanding the importance of defending against and reacting to terrorist violence complements aggressive law enforcement actions.

Military Surprise Attacks and Terrorism

If December 7, 1941 is a day that will live in infamy, September 11, 2001 is certainly burned into the hearts of Americans. Both events held common surprises. For example, both Pearl Harbor and the suicide strikes indicated that America was vulnerable to attack. Both events occurred with no formal declaration of war and both involved civilian casualties. Pearl Harbor and September 11 also shook the soul of the United States.

Despite these similarities, September 11 differs significantly from Pearl Harbor. The purpose of the Japanese surprise attack was to destroy American military capabilities in the Pacific. Japanese governmental and military officials knew the United States would go to war as soon as the surviving Zeros returned to their carriers. The Japanese planned to destroy a military target to support attacks elsewhere, and they knew their action would result in war. By contrast, the September 11 hijackings were designed for drama. The purpose was to murder thousands of victims to create an aura of fear.

Nevertheless, the September 11 terrorists do not consider the actions murder (Lichtblau, 9-29-01). In their minds, strikes against symbolic targets are military actions and civilian casualties hardly represent murder. Civilians associated with the enemy represent combatants (Juergensmeyer, 2000, pp. 143-155). The goal of the September 11 terrorists differed from conventional military strategy. There was no grand offensive to follow the attacks and no notion of a rational, negotiated peace. The terrorists who targeted the United States wanted the West to believe that mass murder can happen at any time. This message is security measures—no matter how stringent—cannot protect citizens.

Defending Symbols and Structures

Asymmetrical war is waged against symbolic targets, and defensive strategies secure symbols. Just because a target has symbolic significance does not mean it lacks physical reality. The bombing of the Edward R. Murrah Federal Building in Oklahoma City in 1995, for example, had symbolic value, but the casualties were horrific. Attacks against symbols disrupt support structures and can have a high human toll. Defensive measures protect both the physical safety of people and property as well as the symbolic meaning of a target (see Juergensmeyer, 2000, pp. 155-163 and Critical Analysis Group, 2001, pp. 9-16).

Greenville Byford (2002) points out that symbolic targets may include civilian attacks. Killing civilians serves a political purpose for terrorists. American citizens contribute economically to the wellbeing of the country, and since they participate in a democracy, they ultimately control military policy. Targeting them, Byford argues, may have practical as well as symbolic value. Rather than engaging in political rhetoric about morality, Byford concludes, it is important to demonstrate that America will not accept defeat. Protecting symbols becomes one aspect of such a strategy.

Ian Lesser (1999, pp. 85-144) outlines three forms of terrorism: symbolic, pragmatic, and systematic. Symbolic terrorism is a dramatic attack to show vulnerability, and pragmatic terrorism involves a practical attempt to destroy political power. Systematic terrorism is waged over a period of time to change social conditions. Although identifying these three forms of terrorism, Lesser points to several examples where symbolic factors enter into attacks. In other words, terrorists use symbolic attacks or attacks on symbols to achieve pragmatic or systematic results.

The University of Virginia's Critical Incident Analysis Group (CIAG) brought a number of law enforcement officials, business leaders, government administrators, and academics together to discuss America's vulnerability to symbolic attack (CIAG, 2001). Symbols can have literal and abstract meaning, such as the case of a capitol that serves literally and abstractly as the seat of government power. The key to security is to offer protection without destroying abstract meanings. For example, the words of one CIAG participant summed up the problem: We want to protect the Capitol building, he said, without making Washington, DC, look like an armed camp.

All societies create symbols and American democracy is no different. In a time of asymmetrical war, American symbols demand protection. The key to security, the CIAG concludes, is to enhance protection while maintaining openness, but every added security measure increases the feeling of insecurity. The CIAG report cites metal detectors at county courthouses. Simply going through the detector prior to entering gives the feeling that all things might fall apart. The irony of security is that it suggests some level of insecurity.

The Institute for Global Education (2001) notes this irony. The Institute assembled a panel of academics to discuss America's reaction to September 11; one of the topics involved enhanced security. Professor Burt DeVries discussed an encounter with security at a Michigan airport. As he stopped at a security gate, the security officer behaved officiously and rudely. DeVries sadly concluded that America was behaving more and more like a police state. The CIAG report warns against this. A democracy, the report concludes, must balance the need for security with general openness to all aspects of public life.

Coordinating a Menagerie of Agencies

State and local police agencies will ultimately decide how deeply they become involved in homeland defense, but the nature of terrorism will force them to participate. When terrorists attack, local police officers are almost always the first government representatives to respond. Even if agencies choose note to develop aggressive counterterrorist intelligence systems, officers will still be called to terrorist scenes as "first responders." When the police arrive, they will interact with a host of other agencies.

American public service bureaucracies have developed several *de facto* roles and missions through historical evolution, and fire departments have inherited several responsibilities over the course of time. They have developed skills in responding to chemical spills, industrial disasters, and urban rescue. New threats brought increased training in nuclear and biological weapons in the 1990s. Firefighters are learning new roles as first responders to terrorism.

Other agencies complement law enforcement and fire department responses to homeland defense. They include the public health community, state-controlled military organizations, and private-sector security. Private companies and public agencies that provide basic services such as power, transportation, communication, information, and other infrastructure services may also have responsibilities. The federal government has recognized the crucial interface between these agencies, establishing the National Infrastructure Protection Center and ordering it in October 2001 to share information among the various entities. The Department of Homeland Security reiterated this call (Office of Homeland Security, 2002).

The defensive role for state and local law enforcement primarily involves responding to emergencies. As in the case of a large industrial accident or a natural disaster, various private and public agencies may assist with the police response. As in offensive operations, the key to reaction is planning. In a major disaster, state and local agencies will find themselves interacting with all levels of government and a variety of other agencies. Preparation for such events need not take place in a vacuum; experience with emergency response planning provides a guide. Furthermore, the federal government has provided extensive assistance with its own plans.

In early 2001 the federal government developed the Interagency Domestic Terrorism Concept of Operations Plan (CONPLAN), involving a system to coordinate the response of six federal agencies to domestic terrorism (CONPLAN, 2001). The agencies include the Department of Justice (DOJ), with the Federal Bureau of Investigation (FBI) as the lead agency; the Federal Emergency Management Agency (FEMA); the Department of Defense (DOD); the Department of Energy (DOE); the Environmental Protection Agency (EPA); and the Department of Health and Human Services (DHHS). By coordinating the response of its major agencies, the federal government hopes to interact effectively with state and local governments after a terrorist attack. The FBI is the lead agency during an attack, while FEMA assumes control afterward.

The federal government originally divided its defensive approach into two different operations: crisis management and consequence management. Crisis management refers to activities occurring while a terrorist incident is taking place. By federal definition, this is a law enforcement activity. While the federal government states that the supportive role of state and local law enforcement is crucial in crisis management, it gives the primary responsibility to federal agencies, specifically the FBI. The CONPLAN speaks about federal cooperation with state and local officers, but it can do nothing to establish a federal-state-local structure. This comes only when federal agencies join state and local agencies in planning, training, and intelligence sharing. Many jurisdictions have taken the initiative to integrate local plans into federal responses. For its part, the federal government sponsors joint exercises and evaluations. The New York City Police Department has even taken crisis management planning and training to a higher level, building a program in conjunction with the Naval War College (Baker, 4-25-02).

Consequence management refers to managing an event after an attack has occurred. FEMA is the lead agency in consequence management, and other federal, state, and local units of government are assigned supportive roles. By its own admission, the federal government has spent more resources in consequence management than in crisis management. State and local law enforcement have followed this trend. This organizational structure is time-tested, and the system has worked in both terrorist incidents and natural disasters. The only problem is that it can do nothing to prevent terrorism. Although effective, it is not a proactive policy.

Not everyone agrees with the idea of dichotomizing crisis and consequence management. A bipartisan committee on national security states that the federal government is spending too much time looking at the difference between crisis and consequence management (Commission on National Security, 2001). In addition, the committee argues that law enforcement will have the lead role in the initial stages of consequence management, so time and effort are wasted by making false distinctions between the crisis and its consequences. Another commission (Cilluffo et al, 2001) advocates dividing the approach to terrorism into two categories, proactive and reactive, and it argues for integrating state and local law enforcement in each phase. The Bush administration recommends ending the dichotomy between crisis and consequence management (Office of Homeland Security, 2002).

State and local law enforcement agencies may utilize federal preparations to assist in planning for responses to attacks The IACP recommends incorporating existing responses in police emergency plans and rehearsing responses prior to an event (IACP, 2001). Ideally, local chiefs and sheriffs will prepare for a terrorist attack by operating in networks and planning to assist one another. The IACP urges police agencies to develop links with fire services, emergency medical facilities, public works, transportation, and federal agencies. It is not a question of either crisis or consequence management, it is necessary to do both, the IACP says, and rehearsing responses uncovers weaknesses. There is also an overlapping advantage in preparing for terrorism. If local departments have planned for a major terrorist event, many of the principles learned in multiagency counterterrorist rehearsals will be applicable to other disasters.

Responding to Weapons of Mass Destruction

One of the greatest threats of modern terrorism involves weapons of mass destruction (WMD). Ian Lesser (1999, pp. 85-144) believes religious fanaticism and the growth of nonstate terrorism help to provide an atmosphere conducive to the use of WMDs. The IACP (2001) warns that WMDs not only cause extensive casualties and damage to infrastructures, they can disrupt communities far from the site of an attack and psychologically devastate an entire country. In earlier times some of the best-known terrorism analysts did not think WMDs were necessarily on the terrorist agenda (Jenkins, 1980, 1986, and 1987). The changing world of terrorism has caused many specialists to rethink the issue (Laqueur, 1999).

Preparation for WMDs falls into several basic categories. Nuclear weapons include both atomic bombs and the dispersion of radioactive materials, so-called "dirty" bombs. Biological weapons involve bacterial microbes and viruses and biological agents are said to be "weaponized" when a microbe is developed in a controllable, dispersible form. Chemical agents are dispersed as solids, liquids, gases, or vapors. They do not last as long as biological agents, but they work more quickly and they are easier to control (IACP, 2001).

Michael Osterholm and John Schwartz (2000, pp. 189-191) argue that the United States has confused the law enforcement response to biological, chemical, and radiological attacks by lumping WMDs into a single category. They are particularly upset by the label "chem-bio," which places biological and chemical attacks in the same category. They are two different types of attacks, Osterholm and Schwartz say, and they require different responses with appropriate types of specialists.

There are parallel skills for each WMD. These include evacuation, triage for mass casualties, containing the incident, and cleanup. All of these activities fall in the consequence management category as defined by the federal government. Yet, there are significant differences with the delivery of each weapon, which require specialized modes of response. One of the primary goals of state and local law enforcement should be to insist that all bureaucracies are prepared to respond to WMDs and are willing to cooperate with other agencies. WMDs represent a massive challenge to state and local infrastructures.

In addition, the role of law enforcement on every level changes in the event of a WMD attack. Law enforcement is not equipped to manage the results of WMD attacks, and it does not have the expertise to recognize the nature of the event. It is counterproductive to try to develop these skills in the law enforcement community because they are highly specialized—often requiring advanced degrees and research—and the knowledge for responding exists in other bureaucracies. Law enforcement has two critical roles in a WMD attack. The police should support agencies responding to a WMD attack and investigate the attack. Investigation will involve teamwork and cooperation among intelligence services and all levels of law enforcement. Responsibilities for assisting other agencies differ with each type of attack.

Responding to Biological Threats

Biological weapons have been used for centuries. Modern arsenals contain bacterial and viral weapons with microbes cultured and refined (weaponized) to increase their lethality. When people are victimized by a bacterial attack, antibiotics may be an effective treatment. In the case of the September 2001 anthrax attacks in Florida, New York, and Washington, DC, public health officials issued preventative antibiotics. Since bacterial agents are susceptible to antibiotics, nations with weapons programs have created strains of bacterial microbes resistant to medicines. Viral agents are produced in the same manner, and they are usually more virulent than bacterial agents and resistant to antibiotics. By the same token, some vaccines issued prior to the use of viral weapons have proven to be effective (see Hinton, 1999 and Young and Collier, 2002).

The problem posed by biological weapons extends beyond the capabilities of all levels of law enforcement. Epidemiologists from the Centers for Disease Control and Prevention (CDC) continually scan disease patterns in the United States to determine whether an outbreak is occurring, but there are serious weaknesses in the system. Osterholm and Schwartz emphatically argue that the public health system is not designed to handle massive casualties produced by a biological attack. The profit motive behind America's public health structure precludes planning for a worst-case scenario. Hospitals are designed to work at maximum cost effectiveness, and physicians are monitored by the amount of patient time they bill. Most physicians are not trained to recognize diseases such as anthrax, smallpox, and plague, and there is no economic incentive for them to gain necessary training. The public health structure does not provide economic incentives to produce hundreds of beds and trained medical personnel who can respond to an exotic biological disaster. Government reports agree (CSIS, 2001 and Office of Homeland Security, 2002, pp. 43-44).

There are four types of biological agents: natural poisons, viruses, various bacteria, and plagues (White, 2003, p. 252). The CDC classifies the most threatening agents as smallpox, anthrax, plague, botulism, tularemia, and hemorrhagic fever. Michael Osterholm and John Schwartz (2000, pp. 14-23) summarize the effect of each. Smallpox is a deadly contagious virus. Past vaccinations are so old that they are no longer effective against the disease. Anthrax is a noncontagious bacterial infection, while plague can be transmitted from person to person. Botulism refers to food-borne illnesses, and weaponized tularemia would probably involve typhoid fever. Hemorrhagic fevers are caused by viruses. One of the most widely known hemorrhagic fevers is the Ebola virus. Bacterial agents can be treated with antibiotics, but the latter have limited or no effect on viral microbes.

America has experienced two notable biological attacks since 1980, and the weakness of the health system was exposed each time. Judith Miller, Stephen Engelberg, and William Broad (2001, pp. 13-33) outline the first modern use of biological terrorism in the United States. Engineered by Rajneeshees of the Bhagwan Shree cult near Antelope, Oregon, the attack occurred in September 1984. (Incidentally, the Miller et al book *Germs* is one of the best nontechnical discussions of biological weapons on the market. It should be standard background reading in American police agencies.)

The attack occurred in two waves as Rajneeshee cultists sprayed food-poisoning bacteria on local salad bars. The attack resulted in hundreds of illnesses, and it serves as a warning to state and local law enforcement. The attack indicated that American police agencies are ill prepared to deal with a biological incident, and the interface between law enforcement and public health fell apart in Oregon. It took a full year for authorities to realize that the outbreak of food poisoning— a wave that overwhelmed local hospitals—was the result of a deliberate action. Even though citizens suspected the Rajneeshees, police lacked the technical ability to investigate the crime, and health officials lacked the skills to conduct a criminal investigation. In short, the police could detect neither the microbes nor the patterns of illness necessary to prove a criminal case, while health officials could isolate the bacteria without locating its source. The Rajneeshee attack begs for a partnership between science and policing.

The second bioterrorism attack came in the wake of September 11. It began in Florida when two tabloid writers were infected by anthrax through the mail. One of the victims died. In the following days, anthrax appeared again as NBC evening news received spores in the mail. Just as in the Rajneeshee attack, there was an initial breakdown among corporate security, law enforcement, and public health personnel. Police and private security officers did not know how to respond, and local public health officials frequently did not know what to advise. The situation grew worse in October.

Then Senate Majority Leader Thomas Daschle's office received its regular mail delivery after lunch on Friday, October 12. Fortunately, staff members were in a class learning how to recognize suspicious packages that afternoon. When staffers returned to work on Monday, they opened Friday's mail. Someone noticed a white powdery substance in a letter. Alerted by information from Friday's class, the staffer took immediate action, perhaps saving many lives. The powder contained anthrax spores. By October 20, Congress continued to function, but it functioned from other locations.

According to reporter Laura Parker (1-23-02), Senator Daschle's workers were exposed to the highest level of anthrax ever recorded. The dosage ranged from several hundred to three thousand times higher than the amount needed to kill a human being. On the day after the attack, nasal cultures indicated the infection was spreading rapidly, infecting seventy-five people, including a pizza delivery person who happened to be present when the letter was opened. Physicians at Bethesda Naval Hospital reserved a number of extra beds in preparation for more infections, but they differed on the way the attack should be treated. They settled on a ninety-day regimen of antibiotics and administering vaccines. Some spores contaminated mail facilities, and two postal workers died after being infected in the government's mail distribution center in Brentwood. The Dirkson Office Building remained closed for three months and cost $14 million to clean up.

Osterholm and Schwartz (2000, pp. 19-20) say anthrax is a particularly effective killer. It is a natural bacterial toxin that has been enhanced by weapons programs. People can be infected eating contaminated food (gastrointestinal anthrax), exposure through the skin (coetaneous anthrax), and by inhaling spores (inhalation anthrax). Inhalation is the most deadly form, but natural spores are so large that the body's natural defense provides quite a bit of protection. Miller, Engelberg, and Broad (2001, pp. 40-44) point to the history of bacterial weapons to show how the effectiveness of anthrax has been increased. Weaponized anthrax microbes are smaller than natural anthrax, and the outside shell is "hardened" so that it can exist in a variety of environments. When the microbes enter a friendly environment, such as the moist tissues of the respiratory system, spores open and begin to multiply.

It is not cost-effective to familiarize law enforcement personnel with diagnostic techniques, but they need to recognize dangers, understand procedures, and know general terms of biological terrorism. A Canadian study demonstrated that one-tenth of a gram of anthrax can infect a ten by eighteen foot room in ten minutes, entering the respiratory system with an amount 180 times greater than a lethal dose (Parker, 1-23-02, p. 6A). A suspected hot zone must be contained, and all people in the zone, including responders, need to be treated. The zone can remain contaminated for weeks unless properly decontaminated.

Rick Weiss, reporting in the *Washington Post* (10-18-01, p. A12), points to several terms police officers should know about anthrax and other biological weapons. Weapons grade means that the bacteria have been finely milled. Virulence refers to the microbe's ability to cause disease, and it is determined by the bacteria's genetic composition. Strains produced in America, Iraqi, and former Soviet labs are particularly virulent. The spores found in Florida, New York, and Washington, DC, were not. Virulence can be enhanced by genetic engineering, a process that transfers strands from one strain of the bacteria to another. Resistance refers to a microbe's ability to resist antibiotics. The Soviets engineered strains resistant to antibiotics. Three types of antibiotics work against nonresistant strains of anthrax: Ciprofloxacin (Cipro), penicillin, and tetracycline.

A report from the Center for Strategic and International Studies (CSIS, Cilluffo et al, 2001, pp. 39-50) argues that biological terrorism is unique. Differing from other WMD scenarios, a biological terrorist attack will involve a period for the disease to incubate, time for it to spread, initial and secondary outbreaks, and efforts to control the spread. The CSIS believes public health agencies must be prepared to recognize and contain all the stages of a biological attack, and they must coordinate efforts with public service agencies. The final CSIS recommendation is to include the FBI in planning. The presence of federal law enforcement necessitates a role for state and local police agencies.

The most important aspect of the law enforcement role in a biological attack is to support the public health system. Local chiefs and sheriffs should have regular contact with public health officials to ensure realistic responses from law enforcement. Quarantine policy, usually outdated in most jurisdictions, is of prime importance in the event of contagious disease. Planners must develop methods for quarantining large areas, enforcing the quarantine, and maintaining security. It is quite possible that officers will be separated from family members who have been exposed to a deadly agent. Law enforcement should also be prepared to assist with the rapid expansion of health facilities into public buildings and to maintain open roads to a quarantined area. Psychologically, officers should be trained to deal with massive casualties. Administratively, some officers will be physically infected and some will be psychologically unable to function. Mutual support pacts—so long a practice in fire services—and clear lines of authority should be established before the event.

It is best to prepare for these events before they happen rather then to simply react. The CSIS (Cilluffo et al, 2001, p. 44) recommends that law enforcement be prepared to:

1. Compel providers to supply stockpiles of antibiotics and vaccines.
2. Be protected from liability for supporting and prioritizing treatment resources.
3. Have the authority to search for biological weapons.
4. Have access to intelligence data.
5. Be given full control of deceased persons.

Osterholm and Schwartz (2000, pp. 183-188) also suggest planning to integrate law enforcement powers with public health, and vaccinating teams of officers for work in hot zones.

Responding to Chemical and Radiological Threats

The massive power and heat from atomic bombs place nuclear weapons in a class of their own, but chemical and radiological attacks are basically similar. Radiological poisoning and "dirty" radioactive devices are forms of chemical alterations. Chemicals are usually easier to deliver than biological weapons and they are fast acting. Radiological devices are slower than most chemicals, but their poison lasts longer and they can be spread like chemicals. Radioactive materials are also more resistant to heat than chemicals, so bombs or other heat-producing devices can be used to scatter them.

There is a good-news/bad-news juxtaposition with respect to chemical and radiological attacks. On the good-news side, American firefighters have quite a bit of training and experience in responding to chemical and radiological incidents. In addition, they know how to contain areas, and they can manage chemical situations more easily than biological attacks. State and local systems have experience in the chemical arena, but not all the news is good. With the exception of large metropolitan areas and jurisdictions with chemical plants, local agencies may not be prepared for chemical and radiological attacks. The reason: training and equipment are expensive (Hinton, 1999 and U.S. General Accounting Office, 1999).

According to the CSIS (Cilluffo et al, 2001, p. 35), Congress attempted to remedy the situation by increasing uniformity in local jurisdictions. The Defense Against Weapons of Mass Destruction Act (popularly known as the Nunn-Lugar-Domenci Act) authorized and provided funding for standardized training in 157 American cities. The only problem with the idea is that several hundred other jurisdictions need to be included. Training and response require expensive equipment.

Apart from the CSIS recommendations, there are two other factors affecting the abilities of local jurisdictions. First, state and local Hazardous Materials (HazMat) teams have experience responding to industrial and transportation accidents involving the spread of deadly chemicals and radioactive waste. In addition, the Department of Defense has quite a bit of historical experience with chemical weapons (White, 2003, p. 251). These factors favor state and local law enforcement as police agencies will generally be used to support HazMat teams and fire departments in the immediate vicinity of a chemical or radiological attack.

Chemical agents come in four basic varieties: nerve agents, blood agents, choking agents, and blistering agents. Radiological weapons would produce short-term burns and long-term contamination and health problems. Nerve agents enter the body through ingestion, respiration, or contact. Blood and choking agents are usually absorbed through the respiratory system, and blistering agents burn the skin and internal tissue upon contact (Organization for the Prohibition of Chemical Weapons, 2000). Radiological poisoning takes place when a contaminated material comes in contact with any source that conducts radiation. The new material, such as contaminated food, water, or metal, becomes an object that could poison humans. Small, contaminated pieces of matter can also become a means of spreading radiation, through the air (U.S. Congress, Office of Technology Assessment, 1995).

Even though public bureaucracies have experience with chemical and radiological agents, state and local law enforcement agencies will optimize planning and operational capabilities when interacting with other departments (Office of Homeland Security, 2002, pp. 41-46 and 55-58).

Police agencies will play a supporting role to fire and health responders in the immediate area of the attack. This means that plans for coordinated responses increase police effectiveness when they are planned, practiced, and revised (IACP, 2001). Law enforcement also needs clear policy guidelines for authority to react and control activities inside and around the scene. The first responsibility is to help fire and medical personnel and evacuate victims. The legal aspects of control must be worked out prior to the attack. The CSIS (Cilluffo et al, 2001, pp. 37-39) recommends realistic training and coordination of state and local efforts.

As with biological terrorism, state and local officers must be trained to recognize the characteristics of chemical and radiological attacks (see Osterholm and Schwartz and CSIS). Even in their supporting roles, the police will be expected to collect and preserve evidence, and psychologically, local and state officers should be trained to deal with mass casualties. Aggressive investigations may prevent other actions. Finally, state and local police must be prepared to enforce martial law.

Before moving to the next section, it is also necessary to briefly mention nuclear terrorism. A stolen nuclear bomb or an atomic blast conjures the worst images of mass destruction. f nuclear terrorism happens, federal authorities will most likely respond with military support. The United States has plans and expertise in nuclear disasters, and the DOD has the monopoly on knowledge. The specter of nuclear terrorism requires old Cold War issue to be resurrected. Law enforcement will play a supporting role, and plans and command structures need to be in place before the event. Response plans will mirror those of a horrid natural disaster.

Law Enforcement and the Infrastructure

A final defensive role for local law enforcement deals with the identification and protection of critical infrastructures. Information, energy, communication, transportation, and economic systems are vulnerable to terrorist attack. Their vulnerability requires law enforcement to develop new capabilities to provide protection. The Department of Homeland Security (Office of Homeland Security, 2002, pp. xi-xii) states that law enforcement agencies will need to develop cooperative links with all agencies involved in defensive measures, including private security. Fortunately, state and local police agencies are not starting in a vacuum. Both governmental agencies and private industry have recognized the need to provide security. In addition, many local chiefs and sheriffs have close relations with business and industry within their jurisdictions.

The Department of Homeland Security applauds efforts to coordinate resources, but critics feel too little is being done. Jeanne Cummings (8-13-02) points to two primary weaknesses. Even a year after September 11, the federal government had failed to release resources to state and local governments. State emergency planners complain they received little federal direction and no federal money. Cummings says the problem is even worse in the private security industry. Conducting a survey of America's largest shopping mall in Minnesota, Cummings concludes that federal law enforcement does little to assist private security. Keeping Americans safe, Cummings says, depends on state and local efforts outside Washington.

Richard Clarke, a Special Advisor to the President with an impressive bipartisan service records, testified before the Senate Subcommittee on the Judiciary on February 13, 2002. He outlined many of the threats facing the nation's infrastructure, painting a grim picture. Most computer systems are vulnerable to viruses, Clarke believes, because customers will not pay for proper protection. The government has opened more communication channels with users and vendors, but more protection is needed. Clarke says the power system and technological organizations are vulnerable to disruptions in Internet grid systems. Pointing to the railroad industry, Clarke shows how many "low tech" organizations have imported "high-tech" support systems. Shut down electrical grids and computers, Clarke maintains, and you'll shut down transportation and communication.

As Clarke stated in testimony, the FBI should not have been the lead agency for infrastructure protection; the role is more suited to technological specialists. (On November 25, 2002, the Bush administration ordered the National Infrastructure Protection Center to move to the Department of Homeland Security.) Extending Clarke's logic, it can also be argued that state and local law enforcement should not play the leading role in infrastructure protection. The key is to develop relationships so state and local police agencies can support security functions.

Protection of the infrastructure comes not with technical expertise equivalent to that of industrial specialists; it comes when specialists in crime fighting and protection establish critical links with organizations serving America's infrastructure. Linkages should be developed in two crucial areas. First, the police should be linked to the security forces already associated with infrastructure functions. The American Society of Industrial Security (ASIS International) has made great strides in this area and more needs to be accomplished. State and local law enforcement agencies must establish formal and informal networks with the organizations in their jurisdictions, and these networks should expand to a cooperative federal system.

Michael Vatis (1999) points to another area. Police agencies need to become involved in the protection of their own information infrastructures. Following the trend in most American organizations, police agencies integrate electronic management and records systems in everyday routines. If these systems are disrupted, police agencies could lose their ability to function. Surveying major agencies throughout the country, Vatis argues that infrastructure defense begins at home.

C. Civil Liberties and Crisis

This excerpt was obtained from Jeremy D. Mayer, 9-11: The Giant Awakens (Wadsworth, 2003).

Civil liberties come under their greatest attack during wartime and crises. While the words of the Constitution do not seem to allow for much alteration during national emergencies, the courts have been far more lenient in interpreting the scope of government power during such times. An act that would be unconstitutional in peacetime may often be upheld in war. In many ways, this is simply logical. Consider the important constitutional principle "probable cause," which limits the ability of the government to arrest and search suspects. The government's suspicions about an odd airline pilot of Middle Eastern descent did not rise to the level of probable cause before September 11; afterward, they did. The Constitution did not change; what changed was the nature of the threat.

Civil libertarians often resist this logic, arguing that it is precisely during times of national emergency when civil liberties most desperately must be defended. When, for example, is freedom of speech more vital than in wartime? When Congress is deciding the appropriate level of agricultural subsidies, the right to criticize the government may not seem to be of supreme importance. When Congress is about to vote on sending young men and women off to die or when the forces of the nation are already engaged in war, the right to object to government conduct may be a matter of life and death. Do Americans lose freedoms precisely at the moment when they most need them?

Civil liberties, as upheld by a watchful judiciary, protect us not only against the government but also against the forces of government and civil society allied together, giving in to the angry moods so common during wars and crises. Other than it its treatment of African Americans during the long horror of slavery and Jim Crow, when has the right to equal protection been more seriously violated in the way communities and the federal government treated Japanese Americans during World War II? During crises, the popular commitment to civil liberties, never as strong as civil libertarians would wish, often falls dramatically. Even in peacetime, many Americans indicate in surveys that they do not believe in the rights of certain minorities to have freedom of speech, whether that minority is pornographers, communists, or the Ku Klux Klan. In war, Americans have even less tolerance for dissent. The elected branches of government may easily be swayed by a popular mood in favor of constricting civil liberties in the name of security. Unfortunately, the unelected branch, the judiciary, may be of little help in crises. As constitutional expert John Frank concludes, "The dominant lesson of our history . . . is that courts love liberty most when it is under pressure least."

In the final analysis, it should be recalled that the preamble to the Constitution ordains that among the first obligations of government are to provide for the common defense, ensure domestic tranquility, and promote the general welfare as well as to secure the blessings of liberty. The idea that the most vital aim of government is the safety of the people is older than our Constitution. In the classic model of social contract theory articulated by such diverse thinkers as John Locke and Thomas Hobbes, citizens surrender certain limited rights to a government in order to receive protection for their persons and property. As the threat to security rises, this may justify government limiting other rights that in safer times are never violated. As *Time* essayist Lance Morrow argued, "A rattlesnake loose in the living room never tends to end any discussion of animal rights." This does not mean that those who zealously fight for civil liberties are wrong to worry about government abuses in crises. In *1984*, George Orwell's brilliant novel depicting a totalitarian future, the state continually justifies its brutal treatment of its citizens by citing war and security threats. Or, as Supreme Court Justice Frank Murphy puts it, "Few indeed have been the invasions upon essential liberties which have not been accompanied by pleas of urgent necessity advanced in good faith by responsible men." In every major crisis in American history, the question of how much freedom we must sacrifice in the name of security has arisen. The civil liberties issues that arose following September 11 were particularly interesting because of the domestic nature of the threat and the new technologies available to both terrorists and the U.S. government.

The Future of Civil Liberties in the Ongoing Crisis

Whenever civil liberties are discussed, opponents of new government limits on individual rights speak of a "slippery slope." They worry that even if new measures can be justified by current threats to national security, these measures may serve as precedents for ominous future encroachments on personal freedoms. Wiretapping that is strictly limited to agents of foreign powers may be expanded to include opposition-party figures, as occurred in other countries and even in this country. Information that the government today gathers for benign purposes may be used by some future government for tyrannical purposes. Once the government starts down a slippery slope, there may be no way to stop the loss of further liberties. For example, the National Rifle Association and other defenders of the rights of gun owners have opposed efforts to license gun owners and register handguns because they fear that such legislation would only be the first step toward gun bans and confiscation.

The attacks of September 11 caused many ideas that had been rejected because of such fears to be considered anew. One example is a national identity card. Such a card could be required either for all residents or only for immigrants and noncitizens. Unlike many nations, the United States has no universally recognized identity card. Passports in America are typically used only for international travel, and driver's licenses are issued by the states and are subject to state regulations. Compared to the proposed national identity card, driver's licenses are easily forged and fraudulently obtained. Indeed, several of the terrorists of September 11 had driver's licenses. Potentially, Americans could be required to carry the national identity card and present it when making major purchases, traveling on airplanes, conducting public business, or entering federal buildings. Identity cards could be encoded with the distinctive record of a physical feature, such as the holder's fingerprints, making them difficult or impossible to forge. This would be very helpful to law enforcement at all levels of American society in the fight against crimes such as credit card theft, fraud, drug trafficking, and income tax evasion. A national identity card would also make it much more difficult for terrorists, as well as other criminals, to hide in the anonymity of American cities and towns.

The government has considered mandating national identity cards in the past to fight such problems as illegal immigration, but these proposals had always been defeated, in part by the slippery-slope concerns of civil libertarians. A national identity card might well put too much information in the hands of the government. Today, a warrant is often required before various government agencies can share information about citizens. For example, the Internal Revenue Service and the Social Security Administration do not make their files on income immediately open to other federal agencies. Civil libertarians worry that a national identity card would be the first step in the creation of a universal data bank containing every aspect of citizens' personal lives. While they concede that it would make law enforcement far more efficient, they worry about the loss of freedom and privacy that would, they believe, inevitably result. The history of data banks held by federal and state authorities offers little comfort to those who worry about privacy and the abuse of such information.

The national identity card has not yet received the support of the Bush administration or any major figures in Congress. It remains on the horizon, along with other civil liberties questions. The attacks of September 11 even raised the issue of the role the military will play in America's domestic security. Since 1878, the Posse Comitatus Act has prevented active-duty military personnel from making domestic arrests or conducting searches on American citizens. At the time of the attacks, the U.S. military had no specific command tasked with defending the borders of the United States except the air defense system designed to monitor Cold War-era bomber and missile attacks. The military now proposes the creation of a new military command encompassing the United States (and possibly Canada and Mexico), raising the specter of domestic use of the massive power of the Pentagon. These fears appear fantastical and overblown to many Americans. Yet few would have imagined how rapidly and radically our government could change before September 11. If another large-scale terrorist attack occurs, the government's power could grow yet again.

Perhaps contractions in civil liberties after September 11 were only natural. Terrorism may be thought of as a disease attacking the body politic, necessitating the ingestion of strong medicine, such as the measures strengthening the power of government to wiretap or to hold detainees without charges. Once the body politic is rid of the disease of terrorism, these measures should be repealed. Yet watchdogs of America's civil liberties, on both the right and the left of the political spectrum, fear that these liberties, once given up, will not easily be reclaimed by citizens. No less an authority than Attorney General John Ashcroft promised that the new era of government surveillance would last for many years. Those who attacked America on September 11 cynically exploited America's open society, its liberties, and its technological prowess to make a sick and twisted protest against the policies of this country. Among the casualties of their evil acts was the breadth of freedom and privacy that Americans had enjoyed as a birthright. Long after the hole in the Pentagon is repaired and Ground Zero in lower Manhattan rebuilt, the damage that the terrorists did to American civil liberties may well linger.

D. Self Quiz About Intolerance

This excerpt was obtained from Diana Kendall, Sociology In Our Times: The Essentials, Third Edition (Wadsworth Publishing, 2001).

True/False

T F   1. Core values in the United States are opposed to racism and a belief in the superiority of one's own group.
T F   2. As a form of popular culture, some rap music has antiviolence and antidrug themes.
T F   3. Some individuals view the Confederate flag as a racist symbol associated with slavery.
T F   4. Some individuals are born with hatred for people who are different from themselves.
T F   5. As the rate of immigration into the United States has increased rapidly in recent years, anti-immigrant feelings have also risen.
T F   6. The U.S. Constitution designates English as the official language of this country.
T F   7. Individuals have been physically attacked for speaking Spanish or languages other than English in public places in the United States.
T F   8. As the United States is increasing in diversity, most dominant group members (middle- and high-income white Anglo-Saxon Protestants) are becoming more tolerant of social and cultural diversity.

Answers

1. False. Among the core American values identified by sociologists is the belief that one's own racial or ethnic group should be valued above all others. Inherent in this belief may be the assumption of racism—that members of racial–ethnic categories other than one's own are somehow inferior.
2. True. Although some people associate all rap music with "gangsta rap," which glorifies violence, drug use, and hostility toward women, other forms of rap music discourage such behavior and draw attention to the severe economic barriers that increasingly divide poor African Americans in central cities from middle- and upper-middleclass African Americans.
3. True. The Confederate flag has become an emotional symbol that continues to divide whites and African Americans in the South.
4. False. Hatred for members of other racial and ethnic groups—like other forms of prejudice and discrimination—is learned from the individuals with whom we associate. It is not rooted in human biology.
5. True. Polls show that high rates of immigration are related to an increase in anti-immigrant sentiment.
6. False. Although the desire to protect the supremacy of the English language in the United States dates back to colonial times, the framers of the Constitution chose in 1780 not to establish a national language. They thought that a national language was inconsistent with the cultural composition of the new nation.
7. True. Individuals speaking languages other than English have been the victims of verbal and physical abuse by individual bigots and members of hate groups, who view such persons as "outsiders who should go back home."
8. False. Recent polls have shown that as the United States has increased in diversity, most dominant group members are not becoming more tolerant. Three examples demonstrate this

point: recent demands in this country that immigration laws be more strictly enforced, renewed interest in establishing English as the "official"
language of the United States, and pressure to eliminate affirmative action programs that might otherwise benefit minority-group members.

Sources: Based on Harvard Law Review, 1987; Herek and Berrill, 1992; Dyson, 1993; and Levin and McDevitt, 1993.

Part V: Political Science Conclusions

Following Operation Iraqi Freedom, several issues continue to be at the forefront of the American response to the events of September 11. Key among them is the "war on terror" and questions about what can be expected in both the short- and long-term in the global fight against terrorism. An essay has been included in this section that aims to provoke further thought on the pressing issues being faced in today's "war on terror." Authors Charles W. Kegley Jr. and Eugene R. Wittkopf examine the state of globalized terrorism and question when and where it all will end in their textbook, World Politics: Trend & Transformation, Ninth Edition *(2004). The second essay is by Maryann Cusimano Love from her book* Beyond Sovereignty: Issues for a Global Agenda, Second Edition *(Wadsworth, 2003).*

A. Can the War Against Global Terrorism Be Won?
This essay was obtained from Charles W. Kegley Jr. and Eugene R. Wittkopf, World Politics: Trend & Transformation, Ninth Edition (Wadsworth, 2004).

In the wake of September 11, a new conventional wisdom has arisen—namely, in the words of U.S. Secretary of Defense Donald Rumsfeld, that "if the [United States] learned a single lesson from September 11, it should be that the only way to defeat terrorists is to attack them. There is no choice. You simply cannot defend in every place at every time against every technique. All the advantage is with the terrorist in that regard, and therefore you have no choice but to go after them where they are." This reflects the view that even if appeasement is tempting, the only way to respond is relentlessly and thoroughly.

A persistent and punitive approach to the eradication of global terrorism is the war on which the United States has embarked, as reflected in President George W. Bush's pledge: "You know, when I first started commenting about this new war, I reminded people that the farther we get away from September 11, the human mind is such that they'll want to forget the terror and the tragedy. . . ."

Exactly what *is* the right thing to do to control the new global terrorism is likely to remain controversial, as President Bush warned. Many experts question his characterization of the problem and the ambitious crusade he promised to undertake, including skeptical allies on whom the United States is dependent if the antiterror war is to be won. *Operation Enduring Freedom* to conduct a worldwide war requires an enduring commitment at very high costs. That is why proposals for an effective and just response to the new global terrorism differ, as do recommendations about how the world can most effectively reduce the probability that September 11 will never be repeated.

What makes counterterrorism so controversial is that strategists often fail to distinguish different types of terrorist movements and their diverse origins and therefore construct counter-terrorist strategies in the abstract—with a single formula—rather than tailoring approaches for dealing with terrorism's alternate modes. As on expert advises, "One lesson learned since September 11 is that the expanded war on terrorism has created a lens that tends to distort our vision of the complex political dynamics of countries" (Menkhaus 2002).

What do you think? If terrorism is the problem, and the goal is its complete eradication, how should those pursuing that quest proceed? In evaluating proposed controls in the fight against the latest wave of global terrorism, you will need to confront a series of incompatible clichés and conclusions: "concessions only encourage terrorists' appetite for further terrorism" as opposed to "concessions can redress the grievances that lead to terrorism" or "terrorism requires a long-term solution" as opposed to the claim that "terrorism cannot be cured but it can be prevented by preemption." Your search for solutions will necessarily spring from incompatible assumptions you make about terrorism's nature and sources, and these assumptions will strongly affect your conclusions about the wisdom or futility of contemplated remedies. Keep in mind that what may appear as policy around which an effective counterterrorist program might be constructed could potentially only exacerbate the problem by provoking the very result your preferred plan was designed to solve: recourse to future terrorist actions. Counterterrorism is controversial because one person's solution is another person's problem, and the answers are often unclear. A counterterrorist program that may succeed in one location may backfire in another.

Consider the diametrically opposed views of whether repression or conciliation is the most effective remedy. Those advocating the former harsh approach see terrorism springing from the rational decisions of extremists to rely on political violence, and they advise prevention and even preemptive strikes that promise surgical attacks to kill terrorists, and failing that, swift and severe retaliation. In contrast are those who see terrorism rooted in frustrations with political oppression and deprivation; they recommend addressing these root causes in order to contain terrorism, taking as their point of departure the November 2, 1972, UN resolution that concluded "measures to prevent international terrorism [require] study of the underlying causes of those forms of terrorism and acts of violence which lie in misery, frustration, grievance and despair." To those of this persuasion, long-term reforms and short-term conciliatory policies are proposed.

At issue therefore is how in fighting the new global terrorism should the line be drawn between the legitimate uses of military force. The debate about methods for waging a just war against the new global terrorism revolves around a series of interconnected issues: Are the policies effective? Ethical? Compatible with other values such as the preservation of civil liberties and democratic procedures? Require multilateral (international) cooperation (or can they be engineered through unilateral, go-it-alone independent national solutions)? Can technology provide a barrier? Can global terrorism be addressed through legal or institutional procedures? What are the relative benefits and costs of counterterrorist measures defined by the categories prevention, protection, and prosecution?

The dangers of stereotypes and the responses they rationalize show why the prospects are dim for eradicating terrorism through negotiated settlements and, conversely, also why combating terrorism through hard military operations tends to legitimize violence and thereby may inadvertently encourage further terrorist actions. The record of past efforts that have relied on these "solutions" reveals their deficiencies. Consider the impotence of promising punitive retaliation to acts of terrorism when those threats are not carried out: "although terrorists attacked U.S. interests more than 2,400 times between 1983 and 1998, the United States responded with overt military action only three times" (Reinares 2002, 92). Although most experts would agree that whereas "it is not possible to extirpate terrorism from the face of the globe," they share faith in the more modest goal—that "it should be possible to reduce the incidence and effectiveness of terrorism." Maintaining a proper balance between respect for freedom and a capacity for decisive resolute action will prove to be a substantial challenge in the "war" against the new global terrorism.

It is unlikely that the danger of terrorism will decline. Indeed, terrorism has become more deadly and harder to curb in the borderless globalized system that makes the practice of terrorism so effortless. The previous reasons for terrorist activity remain as strong as ever, and the information age makes international networking among terrorist groups convenient. The new International Convention for the Suppression of the Financing of Terrorism adopted by the UN in 2000 failed to curb terrorist activity, despite the best of intentions, in and increasingly interdependent world which facilitates the free movement of people and goods across national borders. Adding to the persistent threat is that contemporary terrorism has become more radicalized and more violent. "Any survey of the world map of terrorism—the part of the world where most casualties occur—reveals not only growing fanaticism but also the growth of indiscriminate murder, the desire to exercise power, and sheer bloodlust. In recent years, terrorists have become less hesitant to inflict heavy casualties and cause physical destruction" (Laqueur 2001). As former U.S. Secretary of Defense William Cohen warns, terrorism today is now the work of "cowards who rejoice in the agony of their victims" and are willing to use weapons of mass destruction. Because terrorists now have available a variety of new tactics, such as the use of electronic threats so they can practice "cyber-terrorism" and engage in "Netwar" strategies, the dangers are climbing.

International terrorism is certain to persist for still other reasons. One of the most important and potent is the condition that Walter Laqueur terms postmodern terrorism. This phrase describes the globalized environment which today makes terrorism easy to practice. So-called postmodern terrorism is likely to expand because the globalized international environment without meaning barriers allows terrorists to practice their ancient trade by new rules and methods, while at the same time encouraging state-sponsored terrorism as a substitute for warfare and making the most advanced countries the most vulnerable (Laqueur 2003). Another reason is the rapid spread of new weapons and technology, and their easy transport across borders, which provide unprecedented opportunities for terrorists to commit atrocities and to change their tactics in response to successes in countering them. A third reason is the growing difficulty in a globalized system of detecting and deterring the attacks of disciplined globalized terrorist networks that are generously funded by international organized crime (IOC) syndicates to facilitate their profit in the narcotics trade. And still another reason is the moral ambiguity that surrounds the activities of extremist militia, such as suicide bombers, who are glorified as religious martyrs. In addition, some of the mass media praise terrorists for their independent defiance of government authority.

Terrorists appear destined to be regarded either as hated villains or as honored heroes, depending on the view of the observer. This ensures that terrorism is likely to remain a fixture of twenty-first century politics and that violence will continue to cast its shadow over international relations.

B. Consider the Context
This excerpt was obtained from Maryann Cusimano Love, Beyond Sovereignty: Issues for a Global Agenda, Second Edition (Wadsworth, 2003).

Deciding when to employ what strategy is one of the hardest problems facing government officials who deal with terrorism. There is no single solution. Governments must carefully consider the nature of their terrorism problem in context. Negotiations with those who are perpetrating violence are not the solution to every problem. By the same token, many terrorist campaigns cannot be stopped by military or law-enforcement actions alone. Many people suggest that a decisive factor that determines the effectiveness of law-enforcement activities is the support that the terrorist groups enjoy among their base. Narrowly based terrorist groups can be rooted out, but groups that rely on a broad base of support (some of them from beyond a nation's borders) have a durability that may defy such efforts. For that reason, ethnically based groups may be harder than class-based groups to eliminate through force because ethnicity has proven a stronger ties in most cases.

If negotiations are pursued, then two conditions should be present. First, the government should enjoy a strong popular mandate. Political opponents often portray negotiating with terrorists as "giving in" to terrorism. Such an attack can topple a weak government or, short of that, block whatever agreement has been reached through negotiations. Second, the terrorist organization should be undergoing a period of self-evaluation. In such a circumstance, the government may be able to successfully split off pragmatists from hardline terrorists, bring the population along with the pragmatists, and dry up popular support for those who continue to pursue violence.

Intelligence is important throughout. In confronting terrorism, the nature of the grievance does matter, as does the nature of the organization that puts forth the grievance. Intelligence is important not only to prevent terrorist attacks but also to understand how the organization works and how its decision-making processes can be affected. Because terrorism is global, intelligence becomes an almost intractable problem. How can intelligence collection, analysis, and dissemination be conducted or shared globally? This is resisted by sovereign states.

Terrorism is an international problem and therefore requires politics that go beyond unilateral state actions. Money and weapons flow across borders, and supporters of terrorism (if not the terrorist themselves) often have established bases in other countries. Increasingly, law enforcement efforts aimed at stemming terrorism have an international component, and such a strategy will only require more international cooperation in the future. The nature of the terrorists' grievances matters. Although political violence by itself can rarely achieve its aims, it can sometimes do so in conjunction with less violent political action. By the same token, deterring terrorism and prosecuting terrorists may be insufficient to end terrorism, especially when a large population supports the terrorists' cause. In this regard, the war on terrorism may be as unsuccessful as the war on drugs if efforts to curtail terrorism focus exclusively on military, defensive, and law enforcement approaches. Without addressing underlying factors of what terrorists are fighting for, where they draw their strength from, and how to address their grievances or separate organizations from their base, it will be difficult to manage or end terrorism. The means and targets of terrorism may be global, but grievances are often still local, ensuring that governments will need to use a range of responses to manage networked terror.

Which measures are chosen will depend on the nature of the terrorist threat as well as the domestic political context. The diffusion of power in democratic governments poses a challenge for formulating and coordinating policy.[1] In addition, democracies generally promote the idea of protection of the rights of the individual, bringing pressure on governments to respond to terrorist attacks on innocent civilians. "Democracies can survive the assassinations of leaders. . . but they cannot tolerate public insecurity."[2] However, choosing a response must be tempered by the fact that no democratic regime has ever been conquered by terrorism. Terrorists often miscalculate.

---

[1] Martha Crenshaw, "Counterterrorism Policy and the Political Process," *Studies in Conflict & Terrorism* (Oct. 2001): 329-337.
[2] Crenshaw, "Organized Disorder," 149; Irving Louis Horowitz, "The Routinization of Terrorism and Its Unanticipated Consequences," in Martha Crenshaw (Ed.), *Terrorism, Legitimacy, and Power* (Middletown, CT: Wesleyan University Press, 1983).

Their attacks may rally support for their opponent and strengthen rather than undermine the power of the state. The magnitude of terrorist destruction must also be considered in context. Terrorist destruction "is small compared not only to other forms of political violence such as civil wars or communal rioting but also to other sources of casualties in modern societies."[3] This is particularly true after September 11. The public perception of risk from terrorism generally far exceeds the reality. Citizens in developed countries are more likely to die from firearms or car accidents than from terrorism. Citizens in developing countries are more likely to die from tuberculosis, malaria, or AIDS than from terrorism. The spread of democracy and global media make open societies more vulnerable to terrorist attacks and democracies must be careful not to overreact. In fighting the war on terrorism, we must not become more like our opponents than we would like and less able to address the underlying vulnerabilities and grievances of globalization that can fuel terrorism.[4]

---

[3] Crenshaw, "Organized Disorder," 145.

[4] Cusimano Love, "Globalization, Ethics, and the War on Terrorism," 65-80; Cusimano Love, "Morality Matters," 7-16.